C000181857

PYTHONESQUE

ROY SMILES

Roy Smiles is a playwright from West London.

His many plays include: *Schmucks*, a fictitious meeting between Lenny Bruce and Groucho Marx (Battersea Arts Centre, The Wilma – Philadelphia); the political farce *Roberto Calvi is Alive & Well* (Finborough Theatre) which won a Guinness Fringe Theatre Award; *Danny Boy*, a satire on religion and politics in Northern Ireland (Etcetera Theatre); *The Promised Land*, a V.E Night play written for the fiftieth anniversary of the event (Kings Head); *The Little Green Monkey Club* (Old Red Lion Theatre); an Aids play, *Get It While You Can* – a Conversation With Janis Joplin, a monologue, which won Roy his second Guinness Fringe Theatre Award (Etcetera Theatre); *Stand Up*, concerning Roy's early days as an stand up comic (Old Red Lion Theatre, Edinburgh Festival, Kings Head Theatre); *Bombing People*, a satire on the atomic bombing of Japan (Jermyn Street Theatre); *Ying Tong – A Walk With The Goons* (West Yorkshire Playhouse, New Ambassadors, Sydney Opera House, Court Theatre NZ, The Wilma – Philadelphia, two national tours of Australia); *Year Of The Rat*, about George Orwell's attempts to write *Nineteen Eighty Four*, opened at the Court Theatre in New Zealand in October 2007, its British premier was staged at West Yorkshire Playhouse in March 2008, produced by Michael Codron.

His play about Kurt Cobain and Sid Vicious: *Kurt & Sid* opened at the Trafalgar Studios in London in September 2009.

Both *Ying Tong* and his story of the Beyond The Fringe team *Good Evening* have been broadcast by Radio 4 to critical plaudits.

As an occasional actor he has had regular roles on TV in *Frank Stubbs Promotes* and *Operation Good Guys* and in the cinema played Itzac Heller in Roman Polanski's Oscar winning film *The Pianist*.

He has recorded two albums of original songs: 'Drunks & Dreamers' and 'Winter's Child'. Available to hear on the website: http://roysmiles.selfip.com.

Ying Tong, Year of The Rat, Pythonesque and *Kurt & Sid* are published by Oberon Books.

Roy Smiles

PYTHONESQUE

A Tribute to the Monty Python Team

OBERON BOOKS
LONDON

First published in 2009 by Oberon Books Ltd
521 Caledonian Road, London N7 9RH
Tel: 020 7607 3637 / Fax: 020 7607 3629
e-mail: info@oberonbooks.com
www.oberonbooks.com

A catalogue record for this book is available from the British Library.

ISBN: 978-1-84002-941-3

Cover design by Debra Hutchings Design

Printed in Great Britain by CPI Antony Rowe, Chippenham.

Characters

GRAHAM CHAPMAN
JOHN CLEESE
TERRY GILLIAM/ERIC IDLE*
TERRY JONES/MICHAEL PALIN*
(*These characters to be played by the
same actor)

SETTING
A stage bare save for: a counter, tables and chairs

SONGS
A Mountie Must Always Get His Man

DEDICATED TO
Mike 'Fluffy' Kemp.

THANKS TO
Michael Palin, Mike Kingsbury, Jill Foster, Nick Quinn, all at Oberon, Pieter Torien and all on the South African production.

Act One

A stage in darkness.

Music: lush harps play the 'Theme from Exodus'.

The lights rise during this to reveal a stage bare save for: a counter, some tables and some chairs.

In the darkness the voice of ERIC IDLE is heard, playing a Biblical movie narrator:

IDLE: And so it was Death came knocking and Graham Chapman, friend to all men, finally shuffled off this mortal coil. And behold Death rode a white horse that looked quite perky considering. And, lo, Death was swarthy and had a squint and was a dead ringer for Eli Wallach the bandit chief in the film *The Magnificent Seven*; which is a fine Western as Westerns go but I would advise you to avoid the sequels, which, by and large, suck. And thus Graham Chapman, mightiest and tallest of the Monty Python team despite being considerably shorter than John Cleese, ascended the imitation pine steps, up towards the stars in search of heaven and all its majesty.

And, behold, he beheld a mighty land of cloud where on a clear day you could see the entire universe in all its unbounded infinity – and more cloud. And before him stood the glory and triumph that were the pearly gates, so monumental in their splendour that Graham was moved to use the 'f' word followed by the word 'me' at beholding their sight. And he was humbled. Thence came forth from the gates a great angel, in a cloth cap. And lo, his name was Herbert, and northern was his wrath...

GRAHAM CHAPMAN enters, for the final part of the speech, a pipe clenched between his teeth, quite dead, having just ceased to be;

At the same moment MICHAEL PALIN enters right, playing an officious northern trade union official.

The harp music fades but still plays under the following:

PALIN: Brother Chapman is it?

CHAPMAN: That'd be me.

PALIN: Wondered where you'd got too.

CHAPMAN: Am I late?

PALIN: No clocking on up here, brother.

CHAPMAN: There isn't?

PALIN: Oh no, luncheon vouchers – but no clocking on.

CHAPMAN: So it's official?

PALIN: What's that, brother?

CHAPMAN: I'm dead.

PALIN: As a Dodo: if you can find one.

CHAPMAN: Ah.

PALIN: (*Nodding to pipe.*) No smoking up here, brother, I'm afraid.

CHAPMAN: The pipe? Oh, it's not lit. It's just a crutch.

PALIN: It's just the management don't allow smoking, you see.

CHAPMAN: God you mean?

PALIN: (*Shifty.*) No, the management.

CHAPMAN: Isn't that the same thing?

PALIN: Eh, we're not allowed to say it.

CHAPMAN: What?

PALIN: The word you just said.

CHAPMAN: God?

PALIN: The management, right.

CHAPMAN: Why can't you say it?

PALIN: Blasphemy isn't it? It's in the rule book – Clause Seven.

CHAPMAN: Clause Seven?

PALIN: You can't mess with Clause Seven: 'the management shall hereby be known by the angelic hordes and/or the recently deceased as the gaffers and/or the management'; don't mess with rules that's my motto. Or would be if I had one.

CHAPMAN: So do I just go in, do I, through the pearly gates?

PALIN: If only it were that easy, brother. Unfortunately you have to be judged by the management first. They judge your career and other foibles.

CHAPMAN: Eh – who keeps playing that harp music?

PALIN: In your honour that is, we like to welcome our new arrivals.

CHAPMAN: Do they have to keep playing the theme from *Exodus*?

PALIN: I thought you'd be keen on that one.

CHAPMAN: I played one in *Life of Brian* but I'm not actually Jewish.

PALIN: Oh, I'm sorry. (*Shouts off.*) Cut it, lads. He's not a Hebe.

The music stops abruptly.

Sorry about that. It's your big nose. It threw them.

CHAPMAN: I haven't got a big nose.

PALIN: Keep saying that. One day you might actually believe it.

CHAPMAN: It's a Roman nose.

PALIN: Even Julius Caesar would turn his nose up at a conk like that.

CHAPMAN: Can we get back to the point?

PALIN: (*Surprised.*) There's a point?

CHAPMAN: I mean what happens now?

PALIN: You tell the story of you and Monty Python. I report back to the management. They have a meeting of the sub-committee. Bob's your uncle: if they like you you're in. If not: its hell and all the trimmings.

CHAPMAN: What's hell like?

PALIN: Ever been to Ipswich?

CHAPMAN: No.

PALIN: Less said the better. (*Beat.*) How did it all start then, this Python malarkey?

CHAPMAN: Well, I suppose it all began –

Music: celestial harps strum 'Those Were The Days'.

(*Winces.*) Must we have the muzak?

PALIN: (*Shrugs.*) Clause Five.

A blackout.

In the blackout the voice of a travel film narrator, voiced by IDLE:

IDLE: Cambridge: city of love, learning and gondolas, the mighty pyramids, the hanging gardens of Babylon, more gondolas, Lewisham bus depot, more gondolas and Cambridge University. That Gothic, Norman, Moorish edifice, as designed by the blind Frank Lloyd Wright, standing majestically on a rat infested swamp, dwarfing the town below; educational seat of the three R's: reading, writing and 'rithmatic. Only two of which actually start with an 'R' but you just can't get the staff. First founded by the great Norwegian monarch: Ethelred the Sissy in 937 as a Viking educational facility where you could learn the theory of raping, burning and pillaging without getting those nasty splinters you always get from rowing longboats; there, midst the walls of ivy and the halls of ivy and the gondolas draped in ivy the young John Cleese came to study law, life and laughter.

The lights rise on:

IDLE sitting at a desk, CLEESE enters, IDLE playing his 'Nudge Nudge' character.

Morning, squire, morning.

CLEESE: Hello, I'm a tall if callow student and I'm here to audition for this year's student revue please.

IDLE: 'Course you are, squire, 'course you are. Everyone wants to be in the Cambridge Footlights. To meet the ladies, we all love the ladies. Don't we, chief? The birds, the bints and their bouncy parts, eh? Eh?

CLEESE: Actually there's no women allowed in the Cambridge Footlights.

IDLE: They're not? Oh. Still, got to love the ladies, chief: and their womanly ways, and their curves, and saucy bits, with me, squire, with me?

CLEESE: Not really.

IDLE: Oh.

CLEESE: Can I audition for the Footlights or not?

IDLE: Ready when you are, chief, ready when you are, name?

CLEESE: Actually I'd quite like to change my name for performing purposes.

IDLE: What's your name then?

CLEESE: John Cheese. It's very, very silly. So I'm changing it.

IDLE: Don't blame you, squire. Terrible name: 'John'. It's American for toilet.

CLEESE: I meant 'Cheese.'

IDLE: Nothing wrong with a name like Cheese, squire; look at my name: Idle; silly name that, miles more silly than Cheese; at school they called me 'Bone'.

CLEESE: Is that some sort of sexual reference? If it is stop it at once. I'm from Weston-Super-Mare, where they haven't had sex for years.

IDLE: No, squire, 'Bone' Idle, get it?

CLEESE: Not in the least.

IDLE: What you going to change your name too then, squire?

CLEESE: Cleese.

IDLE: Why not change your name to a cheese?

CLEESE: I'm sorry?

IDLE: John Edam.

CLEESE: No, that would be silly.

IDLE: John Gorgonzola.

CLEESE: Even sillier.

IDLE: (*Quickly.*) John Mozzarella, John Stilton, John Caerphilly, John Cheddar, John Leicester, John Camembert, John Roquefort, John Sage Derby, John Parmesan, John Limburger, John Swaledale, John Brie, John Bath Blue, John Fetard, John Gouda, John Lymeswold, John Shropshire, John Feta, John Goat, John Stinking Bishop?

CLEESE: You're still being silly.

IDLE: Alright then, squire, say no more, Cleese it is. Cleese it is. What you going to do for the audition?

CLEESE: What do I have to do for the audition?

IDLE: Money could change hands, chief, that's all I'm saying; a nods as good as a wink to a blind mason.

CLEESE: Are you suggesting I bribe you to get into the Cambridge Footlights?

IDLE: Only suggesting, squire, strictly hush-hush; you scratch my palm I'll scratch yours. Eh? Eh? Money is the root of all evil only not in this case. Eh? Eh?

CLEESE: I wouldn't sink to anything so immoral.

IDLE: You wouldn't? Oh well. Better have your audition then, squire.

CLEESE: What sort of audition did you have in mind? I have to warn you I refuse to lose my dignity under any circumstances.

IDLE: I had in mind an audition where you lose your dignity under every circumstance – but which doesn't involve nakedness of any kind.

CLEESE: Why didn't you say so? I can do a peculiar walk.

IDLE: Anyone can do a peculiar walk, chief.

CLEESE: Not as peculiar as this.

IDLE: How peculiar can a walk get?

CLEESE: Very, very peculiar.

IDLE: I'll be the judge of that.

CLEESE does an elaborately peculiar walk.

What was that?

CLEESE: A peculiar walk.

IDLE: Oh, I'm sorry I thought you were having an epileptic fit.

The lights cross-fade:

Rising on TERRY JONES, wearing a woman's head-scarf and coat; he addresses the audience speaking in a high-pitched female voice:

JONES: I'm Terry Jones. Mrs. I am also playing Michael Palin, which is confusing to the audience but enough about you and more about me. The first time I met Michael Palin we had a nice cup of tea. And some Spam. I'm very partial to a plate of Spam. I'd say 'Spam' again but I'm afraid of the Python lawyers. They've got the copyright you see. You can say 'pork luncheon meat' in a high-pitched voice but not Spam. Oops, said it again. Back to Michael Palin, who's a very nice man, but I digress, back to Michael Palin, who I was talking about in the first place so it's not actually a digression at all. But I digress. We met at Oxford University, which is like Cambridge University only with better toilet facilities. Yes, we knew how to poo at Oxford. But I digress, back to Michael Palin, who's a very nice man. How about abandoning your career as a round the world travel guru and becoming a comedy writer instead I said? I don't have a career as a round the world travel guru he said, quite rationally. Thus we became comedy writers and wrote many amusing and satirical things, mainly on toilet walls. But there was no living in it. What say you we abandon the toilet walls, I said, and write things down on paper? On toilet paper he said. No, I said, on typing paper. We could lose all our dignity and send it to David Frost. So we did. Within months of leaving college we were writing at the BBC, mainly on their toilet walls but occasionally for *The Frost Report.* Laugh? Not at David Frost we didn't.

The highlight of these writing excursions was meeting Eric Idle. Who was a very nice man but not in the Michael Palin league. Who is? Save for Mother Theresa. Who's a game old bird when roused, though I doubt she's been roused for years. But I digress. Where was I? Oh yes, Spam. I'd love a plate of Spam and a nice cup of tea. But I'm not allowed to say Spam. Python lawyers, they're like vultures, without the beaks, or the need to circle dead bodies in the desert during Westerns starring Randolph Scott. (*Beat.*) I'm allowed to say tea. I could murder a cup of tea – with my bare hands. But the authorities would send me to prison: 'B' wing, Brixton Prison, I'd be the tobacco baron's sex toy and breed budgies like the Birdman of Alcatraz. So, all things considered, better not murder the tea. (*Beat.*) But I digress.

The lights cross fade:

Rising on CLEESE and CHAPMAN sitting opposite one another; CLEESE playing a deranged television interviewer, he addresses audience.

CLEESE: Hello, good evening and welcome to *Haven't We Met?* An in-depth interview show in the style of Michael Parkinson without the mass fawning or sycophancy; I'm speaking to the recently deceased Graham Chapman. (*To CHAPMAN.*) Graham – can I call you Graham?

CHAPMAN: By all means.

CLEESE: Gray –

CHAPMAN: I'm sorry?

CLEESE: Chappers, Chaps, Chappo – the first question we'd all like to ask but I get to ask, as the BBC is paying me an unfeasibly large amount of money to ask it, is how's death treating you, me old china?

CHAPMAN: So far so good except there's a rather annoying northerner says I can't enter heaven until I tell the story of the formation of the Monty Python team in some detail.

CLEESE: Not that I'm interested – however I'll feign interest in respect of the huge fee I'm receiving from the BBC to actually feign interest – but how did you and John Cleese actually meet?

CHAPMAN: Therein lies a tale. Cast your mind back, if you will, to the early 1960's –

CLEESE: I'm sorry we haven't got time.

CHAPMAN: But I've just got here.

CLEESE: Yes, but I spent a ridiculous amount of time at the beginning of the programme on my deeply unfunny opening monologue which means we've had to ask Michael Caine and the Dagenham Girl Pipers to come back on another occasion which only leaves you and you seem to be taking an inordinate amount of time to get to the point.

CHAPMAN: But I haven't even started telling you about how we –

CLEESE: I'm sorry I'm going to have to rush you.

CHAPMAN: (*Panics.*) At college, it was at college. Cambridge. Where they have worse toilet facilities than Oxford but possibly better catering. You were doing law and I was doing medicine but were more interested in doing comedy so we started writing sketches for the Footlights together which didn't have any women in it but I didn't mind as I was a closet homosexual anyway and then we went off to New Zealand to do a review and then we came back and you got a job on *The Frost Report* and you said can I bring my chum Graham and Frost said alright and I started doing that with you and then we did the *At Last The 1948 Show* with the bloke with the bug eyes who later did *Young Frankenstein* with that hump and we developed a cult following and then –

CLEESE: Oh dear, if only you could finish that terribly uninteresting anecdote. But time waits for no man, unless it's me of course; (*To audience.*) next week's guest will be Dame Evelyn Waugh, Pancho Villa, Michael Caine and The Dagenham Girl Pipers. Until then it's goodnight from me and it's goodnight from me.

CHAPMAN: You bastard.

The lights cross fade and rise on:

IDLE as David Frost. He addresses the audience:

IDLE: Hello, good evening and welcome. My name's David 'Ego, Ego show us your legs' Frost and everything is super. You're super, I'm super, *The Frost Report* is super; after the demise of that satirical show of shows: *That Was The Week That Was* I decided to ditch the week that was and put the Frost that was into the title of my next show, swapping more of satire for more of me. Thus *The Frost Report* was a report by David Frost, about David Frost, for the promotion of the personality and career of David Frost. For this I surrounded myself with the leading comic writers of my day. Including many of my former Cambridge Footlights colleagues and the best Oxford University, with its superior plumbing, could offer. Thus within weeks of me David Frost talking to the nation about me David Frost I'd gathered John Cleese, Eric Idle, Graham Chapman, Terry Jones and Michael Palin under my genial if paternalistic wing.

But enough about them and more about David Frost; they broke the mould when they made David Frost. I can say this because I am David Frost. It's not easy being David Frost. It's not easy being right all the time; it's not easy doing a show where you're never off screen. It's not easy being omnipotent but as I'm David Frost and have placed myself firmly on an Olympian pedestal I have to try. They say I built a statue to myself in my own garden but that's a lie. I built it in my own airing cupboard. But let's press on with the story of the Monty Python team in the hope they'll mention me, David Frost, on yet another thirty-seven occasions. This opportunity to address you has been super, you're super but most of all I'm super. So that's a hello from me, a goodbye from you, goodnight, God bless and – super.

A snap blackout.

Lights rise on:

JONES and CLEESE, wearing women's headscarves and coats sitting on chairs as if it were a park bench. They speak in their high-pitched 'pepper-pot' voices.

CLEESE: Monty Python? I remember it like it was yesterday.

JONES: That's because it was yesterday.

CLEESE: Oh, that's right, so it was.

JONES: We all had a nice cup of tea and decided to start a comedy duo, just the six of us.

CLEESE: I remember how it started.

JONES: Who could forget?

CLEESE: How did it start?

JONES: I forget.

CLEESE: Oh, I remember.

JONES: Yes but nostalgia's not as good as it was.

CLEESE: I remember how it started.

JONES: You remember how it started?

CLEESE: I remember how it started.

JONES: Is there an echo in here?

CLEESE: I was standing outside the BBC, minding my own business, slapping passing television celebrities with dead herring – as you do – when Barry Took came up to me.

JONES: Marty Feldman's typist?

CLEESE: That's the one. He was a consultant to the BBC comedy department at the time; aren't you John Cleese he said; yes, I am John Cleese I said, and I claim my five pounds prize and weekend for three at Butlins.

JONES: How did he respond to that slur?

CLEESE: He slapped me with a dead halibut. No, I tell a lie, it was a herring.

JONES: I was attacked by a shark once, on Ealing Broadway, just outside the Odeon; he'd just been to the swimming baths opposite apparently but got ejected by the lifeguard for diving without a snorkel.

CLEESE: Was it painful?

JONES: Save for losing the leg I didn't feel a thing.

CLEESE: Where was I?

JONES: Barry Took, Marty Feldman's typist.

CLEESE: Oh, that's right. Would you like your own television show he said, without the ever deadening hand of the ever deadening David Frost. Yes, I said. But I'd like to bring some people with me I said.

JONES: Attila the Hun's Asiatic hordes?

CLEESE: No, they were out shopping at Harrods.

JONES: The Dagenham Girl Pipers?

CLEESE: No, they were too busy being interviewed on the chat show *Haven't We Met?* Alongside Michael Caine and Pancho Villa.

JONES: Who then?

CLEESE: Graham Chapman naturally.

JONES: The overly butch geezer with the pipe?

CLEESE: That's the one, who I knew from Cambridge –

JONES: (*Wistful.*) – Must have been marvellous going to Cambridge; punting down the Cam in a gondola.

CLEESE: – And Idle, Palin and Jones.

JONES: Sound like a firm of shysters.

CLEESE: We'd survived *The Frost Report* I said, why not survive Barry Took I said? Barry Took took it well.

JONES: What did he do?

CLEESE: Slapped me with a dead herring; no, I tell a lie, it was a halibut.

The lights cross-fade:

Rising on IDLE; he addresses the audience in his own voice:

IDLE: I'm sorry to interrupt the show but this is page fourteen of the script and there's been absolutely no mention of Terry Gilliam. As some of you know having read the over-priced programme I have to play both myself Eric Idle and Terry. Which Terry is not too happy about, are you Terry? (*TERRY GILLIAM voice.*) No, I'm not Eric; actually I'm pretty pissed off. (*IDLE voice.*) So am I Terry, so am I. (*GILLIAM voice.*) I mean Chapman and Cleese have actors each playing them. How come we get the short straw? (*IDLE voice.*) I don't know Terry. It's really unjust. (*GILLIAM voice.*) I mean, you're talking to the director of *Brazil* here, of *Twelve Monkeys, The Fisher King* and *Fear and Loathing in Las Vegas.* All classic movies revered by critics and audiences alike. (*IDLE voice.*) And also the director of *The Adventures of Baron Munchausen,* which lost quite a lot of money at the box-office I believe. (*GILLIAM voice.*) I told you I didn't want to talk about that, the studio ruined that movie with their constant interference. (*IDLE voice.*) Well, you keep taking the piss out of *Spamalot,* despite it being one of the most successful shows in Broadway musical history. (*GILLIAM voice.*) Let's not go into all this now. (*IDLE voice.*) I can't think of a better time. (*GILLIAM voice.*) Are you being snotty with me? (*IDLE voice.*) Are you being churlish with me? (*GILLIAM voice.*) 'Churlish'? Get her. (*IDLE voice.*) Just because we have to share the same actor, it's not my bloody fault. (*GILLIAM voice.*) You want a piece of me? (*IDLE voice.*) Bring it on. (*GILLIAM voice.*) I'm going to kick your ass. (*IDLE voice.*) In your dreams.

IDLE wrestles himself violently.

(*GILLIAM voice.*) Holler Uncle. (*IDLE voice.*) Uncle my anus.

Lights cross fade to:

PALIN, dressed as a member of the Spanish Inquisition, addresses audience:

PALIN: (*Spanish inquisitor accent.*) Yes! I, Michael Palin, dressed as a member of the Spanish Inquisition for no apparent reason, take great offence that I, Michael Palin also have to play Terry Jones, even though he's a charming Welshman who lives in Camberwell, while Cleese and Chapman get actors to themselves, just because they went to Cambridge. But we, the Oxford University graduates, with the superior intelligence and plumbing will be avenged. We will destroy this production from within using the twin weapons of: face pulling, upstaging and corpsing – using the three, three weapons of face pulling, upstaging, corpsing and adlibbing – using the four, four weapons of face pulling, upstaging, corpsing, adlibbing and treading on lines – using the five, five weapons of – I'll come in again.

PALIN exits hurriedly;

The lights cross fade to:

GILLIAM, as himself, addressing the audience:

GILLIAM: Ladies and gentlemen, on behalf of Eric Idle and myself, we'd like to apologise for our childish behaviour. (*IDLE voice.*) You started it. (*GILLIAM voice.*) Not now. (*To audience.*) To return to the story: I'd run into Cleese in New York while he was doing the Cambridge Circus revue there. I was working for the satirical magazine *Help* and I got John to appear in a photo-story as a man who falls in love with a Barbie doll. Typecasting; afterwards he promised to stay in touch. When the magazine folded I thought I'd try London, which was apparently 'swinging' at the time, at least according to David Bailey.

I worked for the *Sunday Times Magazine* and then the *Londoner*, yet another magazine that folded. I had the magic touch. I called John looking for work and he recommended me to the *Do Not Adjust Your Set* guys, a children's show that had become a hit with adults due to Idle, Palin and Jones's performing and writing. Jones and Palin were not keen on taking in a scruffy Yank animator in a kaftan but Eric fought my corner. (*IDLE voice.*) What thanks do I get? (*GILLIAM voice.*) Stop interrupting. (*IDLE voice.*) I want a divorce. (*To audience.*) The guys on *At Last The 1948 Show* were huge fans of *Do Not Adjust Your Set* so when The Great Took suggested to Cleese he make a television show John took most of *Do Not Adjust Your Set* with him. So I ended up, by default, in *Monty Python's Flying Circus.* (*Mock pompous.*) Thus the golden age of comedy had begun –

A snap blackout.

The voice of PALIN is heard addressing the audience like an announcer of a historical documentary:

PALIN: And, so it was a Golden Age of Comedy had begun. Neither bronze nor silver was the golden age but gold. Bright and shiny like a brand new penny or even – gold; and prospectors from all over the land with their stinking armpits, bedraggled beards, lice infested pubic hair and insistence on singing 'Wandrin' Star' dug for that comedic gold. Some found fool's gold: Norman Wisdom, Jerry Lewis or Charlie Drake and were bitter in their disappointment but some found the mother-load: yes, Monty Python. (*Bad American accent.*) And they were rich I tell you! Rich beyond their wildest dreams! Spending their new earned fortune on cigarettes and whisky and bandy legged women! Yee-ha!' (*Normal voice.*) We apologise for that interruption to our normal service. And now on BBC1 this evening's documentary: Yorkshiremen – The Butch, The Bald & The Boring.

Music: earnest kitchen sink drama strings.

Lights rise on:

CLEESE, CHAPMAN, PALIN and IDLE sit in chairs, in cloth caps, speaking in self-satisfied northern accents, in the style of 'The Four Yorkshiremen' sketch.

The music fades.

CHAPMAN: The late 1960's, a golden age of television, not like the rubbish they put on today. People shows? If I want to watch people and be entertained I'll go to my local park and watch juvenile delinquents in hooded tops stab strangers.

PALIN: Aye, they made proper television programmes in those days. *Like Play for Today.* They'd have a miserable play on BBC One about miserable people leading miserable lives and it'd get an audience of eighteen million – and keep those eighteen million viewers depressed for days.

CLEESE: Aye, kitchen sink dramas, those were the days. Some were so miserable they filmed the entire play in an actual sink, with the actors splashing around in the murky water.

IDLE: Dealing with subjects like suicide, despair, homelessness and death by poverty; you just don't get plays on television as entertaining as that these days do you?

CHAPMAN: No, in the 1960's on television you couldn't move for quality entertainment. Like Pinky and Perky, puppets of pigs singing Herman Hermit's hits at high speeds; aye, ribald satire at its best.

PALIN: You had the *Black and White Minstrels*: racist white men with banjos, singing 'Mammy' and 'Camp Town Races' in blackface; you just don't get sophistication like that anymore, do you?

CLEESE: You had *Dr Kildare* – while he was still in the closet.

IDLE: *Champion The Wonder Horse* – before he took steroids.

CHAPMAN: *Flipper* the dolphin – before he took to crack.

PALIN: *The Forsythe Saga* – the costume drama that made wife beating fashionable again.

CLEESE: *Pot Black* – snooker in black and white; watching the grey balls and the slightly darker grey balls being pocketed by chain smoking drunkards: avid viewing.

IDLE: *Bonanza* – the western series about a gay fifty year-old rancher and his three forty-seven year-old sons: always believable.

PALIN: And soap operas: *Peyton Place* with its wooden sets, wooden acting and wooden Mia Farrow.

CHAPMAN: Cop shows: the wooden Ironsides being pushed around by a wooden black actor in a wooden wheelchair.

IDLE: Aye, 1960's television had it all.

CLEESE: News reports from Vietnam showing American soldiers setting light to villages and shooting un-armed Vietnamese. We'd gather round the telly, as a family, and laugh 'til we were blue in the face.

CHAPMAN: And a golden age for comedy too: Benny Hill – a lecherous fifty year-old attempting to grope eighteen year-old busty models in public parks.

IDLE: Aye, tasteful stuff, they don't have comedy like that anymore.

CLEESE: Or the stand up comedians.

PALIN: Balding bigots in tuxedo's telling jokes about black people –

CHAPMAN: The Irish –

IDLE: Or their greasy, overweight mother-in-laws –

CLEESE: Used to make me laugh all the way to my National Front meeting.

CHAPMAN: And Monty Python – lest we forget.

PALIN: Aye, Monty Python: totally original.

IDLE: Totally changed the face of comedy as we knew it.

CLEESE: If Spike Milligan hadn't have done it first it would have been almost groundbreaking.

CHAPMAN: Aye, six bright sparks fresh out of university.

PALIN: Keen to take their clothes off.

IDLE: And dress up as women as frequently as possible.

CLEESE: Introducing a golden age of transvestitism to BBC2.

PALIN: Aye, BBC2: the art channel, with no art on it.

CHAPMAN: Only one thing wrong with Monty Python.

PALIN: Aye.

IDLE: The fans.

CLEESE: Addicts.

IDLE: Obsessives.

CHAPMAN: Boring bastards.

PALIN: To a man.

The lights cross fade to:

IDLE entering and, in the ranting style of 'The Tourist Sketch', addressing audience:

IDLE: Monty Python fans? Don't talk to me about Monty Python fans. Coming over here, taking our jobs; boring everyone silly at their office parties by reciting the Parrot Sketch or the Cheese Shop Sketch loudly, presuming just because they can recite huge chunks of other people's material they are automatically funny when in fact they are the most boring arse-wipes at the party; taking off the music and putting on a record of Live at Drury Lane. Forcing the shy girl from accountants with the pebble glasses, sauce bottle shoulders and small breasts to sing along half heartily to the Lumberjack Song against her will; then putting handkerchiefs on their heads, rolling up their trousers legs, pretending to be Gumby's and beating the balding office manager from sales repeatedly over the head with rolled up copies of the Radio Times; before having their bare arses drunkenly photocopied on the photocopy machine whilst doing clumsy and inept impressions of Eric Idle ranting on about foreign holidays and fat, bloated tourists covered in Boots sun-cream lotion going to Spain to gorge themselves stupid on pint after watery pint of lager whilst –

The monologue is interrupted by a single gunshot; IDLE falls dead.

The lights cross fade to:

PALIN standing with CHAPMAN, dressed in white gowns, as the opening scene.

PALIN playing the officious northern official; CHAPMAN playing the recently deceased comedian.

CHAPMAN: Is this it then?

PALIN: What brother?

CHAPMAN: A series of interrelated sketches in the style of Monty Python?

PALIN: Might be.

CHAPMAN: But it's hardly theatre is it?

PALIN: What were you expecting, Hamlet?

CHAPMAN: Something a little more dignified.

PALIN: How do you mean?

CHAPMAN: This is supposed to be about my death; where are the dramatic turns, the tears of a clown pathos, the heart wrenching melodrama?

PALIN: Come to the wrong place for that, brother.

CHAPMAN: I want to complain.

PALIN: Who too?

CHAPMAN: God.

PALIN: (*Evasive.*) You mean the management?

CHAPMAN: Alright then, the management.

PALIN: Can't do that.

CHAPMAN: Why not?

PALIN: It's Yon Kippur.

CHAPMAN: Are you telling me God is Jewish?

PALIN: (*More evasive.*) Possibly.

CHAPMAN: I demand to speak to someone in higher authority.

PALIN: Well, there is a complaints department.

CHAPMAN: That'll do. How do I get there?

PALIN: It's over there, just by the actor playing John Cleese.

CHAPMAN: Right, I'll soon put a stop to this silliness.

The lights cross fade to:

CLEESE sits at a desk. With a sign: 'Complaint's Department' written on it.

CHAPMAN enters the scene.

Is this the complaints department?

CLEESE: No it's not.

CHAPMAN: But it says so on the door.

CLEESE: No, it doesn't.

CHAPMAN: And there's a sign there on your desk that says: 'Complaints Department.'

CLEESE attempts to cover the sign with his arm.

CLEESE: No, there isn't.

CHAPMAN: I can see it.

CLEESE: No, you can't.

CHAPMAN: You're trying to hide it with your arm.

CLEESE: Oh, so there is. Very well, what can I do for you?

CHAPMAN: I want to complain about this theatrical experience.

CLEESE: What about it?

CHAPMAN: It's not a theatrical experience.

CLEESE: It could be.

CHAPMAN: Telling the Monty Python story using silly sketches is hardly theatre is it?

CLEESE: Define theatre. We're on a stage aren't we?

CHAPMAN: Theatre's not just a stage. Theatre should be a moving experience, something that touches you.

CLEESE: I'm moved.

CHAPMAN: By what?

CLEESE: (*Lost.*) Eh –

CHAPMAN: You're not moved at all.

CLEESE: Well, theatre is a broad church isn't it?

CHAPMAN: Define 'broad church'.

CLEESE: Well, for instance, in the 70's, you could have a naked mime troop recreating the American Civil War using glove puppets and people would still go and see it. They called anything 'theatre' in those days.

CHAPMAN: This isn't the 70's.

CLEESE: But that it was. We'd get a grant.

CHAPMAN: You're avoiding the point.

CLEESE: How can I avoid a point when you haven't made one?

CHAPMAN: My point is: this is just a meaningless comedy.

CLEESE: By definition all comedy is meaningless.

CHAPMAN: On the contrary: comedy can bring down tyrants; laughter is the first tool of the bloodless revolution.

CLEESE: Right, the satirical cabarets of the Weimer Republic laughed Hitler right out of office didn't they? You couldn't move for laughs in the salt mines of Russia but it didn't bring Stalin down did it?

CHAPMAN: Well, whatever, I want this show to have more gravitas.

CLEESE: (*Hopeful.*) I could wear a beard.

CHAPMAN: Now you're being silly.

CLEESE: Silliness is the point. The Monty Python team abandoned the satirical drive of *Beyond the Fringe* and struck out in a more surrealist direction. But we were still, in our own way, attacking the constraints and the repressions of English society.

CHAPMAN: That's all very well. But I demand we get back to the tragic and moving story of a man wrestling with his considerable demons.

CLEESE: Who's that then?

CHAPMAN: Me.

CLEESE: Still not with you.

CHAPMAN: Graham Chapman.

CLEESE: (*Surprised.*) You're playing Graham Chapman?

CHAPMAN: Yes.

CLEESE: Why didn't you say so?

CHAPMAN: Who did you think I was playing?

CLEESE: One of the chaps who have to double up, it's so confusing.

CHAPMAN: This sketch is going nowhere.

CLEESE: Well, we haven't got Gilliam's animation to bail us out.

CHAPMAN: Better get back to the story.

CLEESE: (*Worried.*) There's a story?

The lights cross fade to:

JONES sits in a woman's coat and wearing a long blonde wig. He addresses the audience, speaking in his high pitched 'pepper-pot' voice:

JONES: Hello, I'm Carol Cleveland. The blonde bint that was in all the Python television shows; four series I did but do I ever get a mention in the biographies? Do I bollocks. Year after year after year I worked for them. Listening to Cleese moaning about the catering and Chapman droning on about gay liberation and Eric Idle going on and on about playing ping-pong with George Harrison and Palin waxing lyrical about steam trains and Thomas The Tank Engine and whatever happened to the Flying Scotsman and Jones harping on about Viking mythology, medieval cutlery in the Dark Ages and how hard it was growing up Welsh in Surrey and what thanks do I get? Bugger all. Just the usual stingy BBC pay packet and sling your hook, dear. They never liked women in Monty Python. They preferred dressing up as birds themselves. Oxbridge graduates: transvestites to a man. No wonder this country has gone to pot. Well, they run the country don't they?

Labour, Tories, the BBC, the whole establishment is one big playground for Oxbridge graduates to ponce about in; come the revolution, that's what I say. They'll be women on every comedy programme. And they'll get more than one line an episode and have to flash their tits. (*Tuts*.) Did Germaine Greer burn her Australasian bra in vain? Probably. (*Beat*.) I could murder a cup of tea.

A snap blackout, lights rise on:

IDLE enters as travel journalist Alan Whicker, carrying a microphone and addressing the audience:

IDLE: But we leave behind these wind tossed and sun blighted shores of dearest, dearest England in search of sunnier shores and the travel documentary guru that is: Michael Palin –

Enter CHAPMAN as Alan Whicker, carrying a microphone and addressing the audience:

CHAPMAN: Yes, for once where the BBC used to send myself Alan Whicker to far-flung shores in search of sun kissed places and sun kissed people –

Enter CLEESE as Alan Whicker, carrying a microphone and addressing the audience:

CLEESE: Now they send Michael Palin. Comedian, humourist and humanitarian; is there any part of the world this mild mannered yet endearing travel guru has not travelled?

IDLE: From the highs of the Himalayas –

CHAPMAN: To the lows of the Netherlands –

CLEESE: From pole to pole –

IDLE: North to south –

CHAPMAN: East to west –

CLEESE: And back again.

IDLE: Walking where no white man has ever walked.

CHAPMAN: And where no black man would ever want to go.

CLEESE: Swapping platitudes with yak herdsmen from Nepal.

IDLE: Or puns with llama salesman from Peru.

CHAPMAN: Debating Stalinism with Slovakian cheese grinders.

CLEESE: Or Satanism with sheep rustlers from Wallamaloo.

IDLE: Where once I, Alan Whicker, would ask fascinating yet never patronising questions of the exotic or the fanciful –

CHAPMAN: Now I Alan Whicker remain behind in the retirement home for travel guru's whilst Michael Palin –

CLEESE: A very nice man from Sheffield gets to travel the world –

IDLE: On behalf of the BBC –

CHAPMAN: And ask pertinent questions –

CLEESE: Of other lifestyles –

IDLE: And other peoples.

CHAPMAN: But what lies behind the mask?

CLEESE: What demons fester?

IDLE: What exactly is the nice Michael Palin hiding and why does he keep travelling vast distances to hide it?

CHAPMAN: Tonight I Alan Whicker –

CLEESE: In a fascinating, behind the scenes insight –

IDLE: Go in search of the real Michael Palin –

CHAPMAN: In a documentary entitled –

IDLE, CLEESE & CHAPMAN: Will The Real Michael Palin Please Stand Up?

The lights cross fade to:

PALIN sitting at a desk, reading from his diary:

PALIN: Extract from the Michael Palin diaries. February 14th. Woke up, was nice to the wife, went downstairs, was unfeasibly nice to the children, went out into the garden, nearly stood on a snail. Put the snail gently on to some grass. As it went on its way it waved; ran into the milkman, he insisted I had free milk, eggs and yoghurt again, kissed me on both cheeks and left. The postman was passing. Ran over, hugged me, burst into tears and sobbed: 'they broke the mould when they made you'.

Realised I was in for another day of nice hell. 15th February. Got up, decided I had to break out of the chains of niceness, was tart and arch to the wife, she laughed, ruffled my hair and ran me a nice hot bath; went downstairs, was surly and aggressive to one of the children, he giggled, punched me affectionately in the stomach and ran into the front room tittering, curses; saw another snail in the garden, ran out with some salt, eager to cruelly destroy, couldn't do it, poured the salt over my own head instead; became enraged by my own decency and humanity, nipped next door and tried to strangle their budgie, couldn't do it, ended up with the budgie on my shoulder, stroking my ear with its wing, whilst trilling thirteen verses of Zipper-Dee-Doo-Da. Double curses. 16th February. Woke up even more determined to be nasty, cruel and nice no more; went to a Python meeting at Jones's house in Camberwell. Attempted to run over Terry Gilliam's foot as I arrived, he wept with laughter and told me I was the funniest man alive; went inside for script conference, casually tried to stab Graham Chapman in the eye with a pencil. He guffawed wildly and swiped me genially 'round the head with his pipe. Wrestled Eric Idle to the ground and attempted to give him a rather nasty Chinese Burn. He belly laughed so hard he almost wet himself; said mean and cutting things to Cleese. He responded by kissing me full on the mouth; attempted to set light to Jones' house by pouring paraffin over the curtains. Jones found this so amusing he ran off to get some fire-lighters to join in; returned home defeated, went out into the garden, stared up at the stars and shook my fist at malignant gods: 'why am I cursed by this niceness, lord, why me?' Went indoors, had a nice cup of tea, nipped out, filmed an entire round the world travel documentary retracing the steps of Marco Polo in one evening and thus – to bed.

A snap blackout.

Music: cheese game-show organ music plays.

The lights rise on:

CLEESE playing a very slick and insincere game show host in a glittery jacket and bow tie. He addresses the audience:

CLEESE: Hello and welcome to that quiz of quizzes: *Patronising the Proletariat*. The ITV quiz that gives points and what do points make? That's right, ladies and gentlemen, prizes. First prize is a night in Las Vegas watching Englebert Humperdink in concert. Second prize is two nights in Las Vegas watching Englebert Humperdink in concert. Third prize is the Turin Shroud. Dry clean only: not machine washable. But let's meet our first member of the proletariat – come on down, Mr. Clumpy.

CHAPMAN enters as a contestant.

You are Mr Norbert Clumpy of Eastleigh Close, Devizes, Wiltshire?

CHAPMAN: My brain hurts.

CLEESE: Of course it does and thank you for sharing. And what are you answering questions on tonight Mr Clumpy?

CHAPMAN: *Monty Python's Flying Circus*: 1969-1974.

CLEESE: Of course you are. On with the questions because what do questions make?

CHAPMAN: Prizes?

CLEESE: Of course they do, Norbert, of course they do. First question Mr Clumpy: who wrote the 'Liberty Bell' theme tune to the Monty Python series? Was it a) Debussy b) Rasputin the Mad Monk or c) Sousa?

CLEESE: Sousa?

CLEESE: That's correct, Mr Clumpy. Rasputin the Mad Monk, of course, wrote the theme tune to *The Saint*. Second question: the first broadcast of Monty Python went out in the supposed 'God Slot' on Sunday 5th October, 1969. Which leading Hollywood actor – not Charlton, Heston, not Charlton Heston – most resembles God?

CHAPMAN: Eh – Christopher Plummer in *The Sound Of Music*?

CLEESE: Correct, Mr Clumpy, you're not as stupid as you look but that would be very, very hard. (*Beat.*) The next question is a trick question, Norbert. It was the second episode made but the first episode to be broadcast. What was the name of that very first broadcast?

CHAPMAN: Wither Canada?

CLEESE: That's correct, Mr Clumpy. Canada: where men are men, women are women and backward children take up ice hockey. Next question: save for moose wrestling and excessive flatulence Canadians are famous for what, for what?

CHAPMAN: Having very gay Mounties?

CLEESE: That's correct. But let's press on. 'Python' means what? 'Python' means what?

CHAPMAN: In Greek mythology: it's the huge serpent or monster killed by Apollo near Delphi. In Late Latin it's a familiar or possessing spirit; or, generally, a large non-venomous snake of the family Pythonidae.

CLEESE: A dull answer, a tedious answer, but the correct answer; next question: the Scottish singer Lulu, whose hits include: 'Boom-Bang-A-Bang', 'I'm A Tiger' and 'To

Sir With Love' was a guest on series four. Lulu was once married to Maurice Gibb. Maurice Gibb was a member of the Bee Gees. The Bees Gees had a hit in 1967 with 'New York Mining Disaster'. New York, New York was so good they named it twice. *You Only Live Twice* was the only Bond movie to be scripted by Roald Dahl. Roald Dahl is the silliest name in the library save for Edgar Lustgarten. Edgar Lustgarten was the pseudonym for Wolverhampton Wanderers midfield maestro Billy Wright. Billy Wright's favourite television series was *Rawhide*. Frankie Lane sang the theme tune to *Rawhide* and also the theme tune to *Champion the Wonder Horse.*

Champion the Wonder Horse was on steroids. The entire East German ladies shotput team at the 1970 Olympic Games in Mexico were on so many steroids they grew testicles. Mexico is the home of the revolutionary Pancho Villa, who appeared as a guest on the chat show *Haven't We Met?* With Michael Caine and the Dagenham Girl Pipers; Michael Caine was in the film *The Italian Job.* Here's the question: which cast member of *The Italian Job* famously declared he'd like to: 'give Lulu a good seeing too,' 'give Lulu a good seeing too'?

CHAPMAN: Eh – Benny Hill?

CLEESE: Is correct, Mr Clumpy. Next question: John Cleese once famously hid Graham Chapman's deeply significant pipe as a prank. Chapman kneed him very, very forcefully where? Where?

CHAPMAN: In the genitals?

CLEESE: Is the correct answer, you're doing well, Norbert, you have the Turin Shroud; you have the two nights in Las Vegas watching Engelbert Humperdink. Final question, Mr Clumpy, for only one night watching Engelbert Humperdink in concert: what reason did John Cleese give for leaving the show after series three, what reason did John Cleese give for leaving the show?

CHAPMAN: (*Stumped.*) Eh –

The lights cross fade:

ERIC IDLE stands holding a BAFTA style statue and speaks to the audience in tear-soaked, showbiz, over earnestness – in the style of Lord 'Dickie' Attenborough:

IDLE: Ladies, gentlemen and your most royal highness, good evening, it's my very great privilege to give this award tonight for services to the comic arts to a very, very special person: John Marwood Cleese. Born in the slums, nay, the ghetto that was Weston-Super-Mare John has risen about his Shanty Town and pimp haunted roots to become a veritable giant of British comedy. Surviving the freakish abnormality of his height, dandruff, and having to appear with Tommy Steele, a right berk by all accounts, in the Broadway production of *Half A Sixpence.* Imagine the self-loathing, despair and general hell of having to return to Britain in order to work with David Frost. But this John did in search of that Holy Grail that was comic perfection. Imagine then his horror at having to work with Oxford graduates on Monty Python, continually boasting about their superior shit-houses, and also, alas, an American. (*Water starts squirting out of his eyes.*) Picture if you can the desperate, bitter unhappy years when he was forced, against his will, to play authority figures and men who did peculiar walks all to make an unforgiving nation laugh. Finally he escaped the narrow confines of being in one of the most successful and wildly imaginative television shows of all time to go off to make *Fawlty Towers*: a shabby, second rate programme that paled into squalid insignificance alongside the comedic giant that was *Rutland Weekend Television,* made by Eric Idle, which the narrow minded fools at the BBC still refuse to repeat, but I digress. Unfortunately John can't be with us here tonight as he's busy washing his hair but I'd like to accept this award on his behalf. Greater than Gandhi, taller than Churchill and whiter than Martin Luther King let us all grovel before the temple that is the genius of John Cleese; the man who

turned his back on being named after one of the great
cheeses of our time; John, you're with us in spirit if not
the flesh. The flesh is weak, the dollar is mighty but in the
streets of heaven tonight the angels will bawl your name.
(*Sinks to his knees, sobbing unfeasibly.*) God, I love being in
showbiz.

A snap blackout.

The voice of CLEESE is heard in the darkness:

CLEESE: The BBC would like to apologise to Richard
Attenborough for the former sketch. In no way do they
believe Mr Attenborough to be an over-gushing, fawning
nit; or, at least, not the first two. (*Breezy.*)

His brother, Sir David of course, is the famous naturalist.
Oft to be seen groping gorillas in their natural habitat;
ah, to grope a gorilla now that spring is here. If you tickle
an Orang-utan they get erect straight away, you know.
Monkeys have been scientifically proven to masturbate
thirty seven times a day, which is three times more than
the average Conservative apparently; ah, to fondle a Tory
now that summer is here; if you play the National Anthem
they get erect straight away, you know; but now for
something – slightly – different.

Lights rise on:

*CLEESE, PALIN, CHAPMAN and GILLIAM; CLEESE sits (doing his
Reg' voice from* Life of Brian*). The others stand.*

I'm leaving the show, I've had enough, I'm through, I'm
pissed off, I've had it. After all, what have the BBC ever
done for us?

PALIN: Gave us our own television series?

CLEESE: Alright, I'll give you that, but bar giving us our own
television series what have the BBC ever done for us?

CHAPMAN: Put us on the cover of the Radio Times?

GILLIAM: Paid us handsome salaries?

PALIN: Made us internationally known superstars?

CLEESE: Alright, alright, fair point, they've given us our own television series, put us on the cover of the Radio Times, paid us handsome salaries and made us internationally known superstars but bar that, what have the BBC ever done for us?

CHAPMAN: Allowed us to express our artistic freedom without too much interference from above?

PALIN: Gave us a very reasonable time slot?

GILLIAM: Put us forward for an award at the Montreaux comedy festival?

CHAPMAN: Allowed us all the rehearsal time necessary?

PALIN: Furnished us with very generous catering facilities?

GILLIAM: Invited us to the annual glittering staff dinner, dance and reception?

CLEESE: Alright, but bar giving us our own television series, putting us on the cover of the Radio Times, paying us handsome salaries, making us internationally known superstars, allowing us to express our artistic freedom without too much interference from above, giving us a very reasonable time slot, putting us forward for an award at the Montreaux comedy festival, allowing us all the rehearsal time necessary, furnishing us with very generous catering facilities and inviting us to the annual glittering staff dinner, dance and reception, what have the BBC ever done for us?

CHAPMAN: Gave us complimentary tickets for *Come Dancing*?

CLEESE: Oh fuck off.

A snap blackout.

In the darkness the voice of GILLIAM:

GILLIAM: Hi, I'm Terry Gilliam and I'd just like to take a moment to apologise for all the swearing in the show so far. I come from the States where swearing is frowned upon and we're all good, God fearing, Church going people. You wouldn't catch us swearing like you atheistic Brits. You guys swear like mother – (*A loud bleep.*) Oh, I'm sorry, I said mother – (*A loud bleep.*) Ooops, I said it again. I do apologise, on with the (*A loud bleep.*) show; two (*A louder bleep.*) arguing in a pet shop. (*Dramatic voice.*) Or are they? (*Beat.*) Yep, they are.

The lights rise on:

PALIN standing behind a counter looking very working class and shifty; CLEESE enters carrying a (huge) stuffed budgerigar in a cage. He approaches the counter.

CLEESE: Is this the shop I bought this very budgerigar from not thirty minutes ago?

PALIN: (*Scoffs.*) Budgerigar?

CLEESE: (*With heavy emphasis.*) Yes, budgerigar.

PALIN looks bemused.

CLEESE: (*Hisses.*) Python lawyers.

PALIN: (*Aside.*) Oh, right. (*Louder.*) Might be, I suppose you want a refund?

CLEESE: On the contrary, I'm returning to this shop to congratulate you.

PALIN: Congratulate me?

CLEESE: This is without doubt the finest budgerigar I have ever owned. It can speak five languages, including Hindustani, tap dance, play piano to concert hall level, sing the Hallelujah Chorus, sometimes in Latin, and complete the *Times* crossword in less than seven minutes. It's the best pet I've had in thirty-five years of bestriding this island earth.

PALIN: Yeah, but it looks a bit peaky, better give you a refund.

CLEESE: It is not peaky.

PALIN: Yes, it is, it looks all clapped out.

CLEESE: It's just sung the 'Hallelujah Chorus' in Latin whilst tap-dancing. You'd be clapped out, mate.

PALIN: Its feathers look all mouldy, and it's gone green look.

CLEESE: It's a green budgerigar, what colour is it supposed to look like? It's not an iguana, changing its colour on a whim every two bleeding minutes.

PALIN: And its droppings are all discoloured.

CLEESE: Your droppings are probably discoloured, there's no dignity in droppings my good man.

PALIN: Nah, it's at death's door, better give you a refund.

CLEESE: I don't want a refund.

PALIN: I could swap it?

CLEESE: Where are you going to find another budgerigar that can play the Brandenburg Concerto on the ivories whilst translating Noël Coward motifs into Hindustani? It's not going to happen, my good man.

PALIN: But it's poorly –

CLEESE: This budgerigar is not poorly. It is in the pink, full of vim and vigour, downright perky, hunky dory, in tip top condition, filled with the joys of spring, if it were Irish it'd be on top of the morning; this budgerigar could pass a physical for the SAS, it's so healthy it's applied to join a gym, it's one hundred per cent, A1, feeling groovy; to conclude it's the fittest budgerigar east of Java, north of the equator and south of the Pecos.

PALIN: Go on, let me buy it back.

CLEESE: Why do you want it back?

PALIN: I miss him. Well, he's my common law wife.

CLEESE: Common law wife?

PALIN: We would have got married but those bigoted swine in the Anglican Church wouldn't let us have the religious ceremony. They say it's in the Bible: 'man shall not lie down with a budgerigar and be fruitful'.

CLEESE: Then why'd you sell him to me not half an hour ago?

PALIN: We had a row about his crackers. He said some pretty hurtful things in Hindustani; I responded with some unsavoury comments in Latin, but it was the heat of the moment, we're in love.

CLEESE: This budgie doesn't know you from Adam.

PALIN: Yes, it does. Look, he just blew me a kiss.

CLEESE: No, he didn't.

PALIN: Well, he winked.

CLEESE: You liar.

PALIN: Pouted then.

CLEESE: Budgerigars do not pout. How can you pout with a beak?

PALIN: When you're in love anything is possible.

CLEESE: Wait a minute, how is doing a pastiche of their most famous sketch progressing the story of the Monty Python team?

PALIN: It's reverential.

CLEESE: Reverential is all very well but we've been here before haven't we? They're right what they say: 'repetition is the mother of desperation'.

PALIN: (*Beat.*) Who says that then?

CLEESE: Whoever said it first.

PALIN: But you said 'they' like you knew them.

CLEESE: I don't know everyone called 'they.' That would be an infinite number of people.

PALIN: But by the very suggestion 'they say' would be the inference that you actually knew who 'they' were.

CLEESE: No it wouldn't.

PALIN: Yes it would.

CLEESE: Now you're playing Devil's Advocate, just to take up a contrary position.

PALIN: No I'm not.

CLEESE: Yes you are.

PALIN: I'm making a perfectly valid point about the absurd conversational over-use of the expression 'they.'

CLEESE: This is ridiculous; this is supposed to be a parody of the parrot sketch.

PALIN: No its not.

CLEESE: Yes it is.

PALIN: On the contrary.

CLEESE: I can prove it.

PALIN: No you can't.

CLEESE: What am I doing with this budgerigar then?

This throws PALIN for a moment then:

PALIN: You might have secreted that budgerigar about your person to reveal at a precise conversational moment merely to win the right to utter 'they say' whenever the occasion demands it without the intellectual validity of its actual usage.

CLEESE stares, a long pause.

CLEESE: Say that again.

PALIN: I would if I could but I can't.

An embarrassed silence.

CLEESE: That's the end of the sketch is it?

PALIN: Looks like it.

CLEESE: Righto.

CLEESE begins to shuffle off stage with the budgerigar looking embarrassed.

FX: the budgerigar begins to sing: the 'Hallelujah Chorus' enthusiastically.

CLEESE: (*Hisses.*) Not now, not now.

He exits. A snap blackout;

In the darkness the voice of IDLE is heard, playing the Canadian film actor Christopher Plummer:

IDLE: Good evening. My name is Christopher Plummer. I was Captain Von Trapp in the musical *The Sound of Music.* And, yes, I look like God. I am a Canadian and I sincerely believe, in my heart of hearts, that God is a Canadian. I take great exception to the previous references about Canadians having homosexual Mounted Police, wrestling moose and suffering from excessive flatulence. (*Beat.*) But I digress. Famous Canadians include Neil Young, Joni Mitchell and William Shatner.

Our major exports are maple syrup and wheat, endless fields of wheat, wheat as far as the eye can see. I get moist just thinking about that wheat. (*Sings to the tune of 'Edelweiss'.*) 'Canada, Canada every morning you greet me – '

This monologue is interrupted by the sound of a hand grenade exploding;

Lights rise on:

CHAPMAN and PALIN stand dressed in white, before the pearly gates.

CHAPMAN: I've had enough of this – I'm going in.

PALIN: Can't do that, brother, the management are peeved at you as it is.

CHAPMAN: Peeved? Was it the chronic alcoholism? I conquered that. Alright, I used to whip out my tadger in public bars and dunk it in other people's Gin & Tonics but that was the drink talking.

PALIN: I can sum up their objections in three words: *Life of Brian.*

CHAPMAN: What was wrong with it?

PALIN: It was a patent attack on Christianity.

CHAPMAN: It was an attack on intolerance and religious zealotry.

PALIN: What's the difference?

CHAPMAN: The difference is the Pythons liked Christ. He promoted peace, love and understanding. Why would the Python team be anti that? We never actually practiced peace, love and understanding amongst ourselves but we weren't technically against it.

PALIN: Well, the film was banned in Norway.

CHAPMAN: Oh, that's your moral barometer is it? If it's banned in Norway it must be wrong? They've banned smiling in Norway. It's got the second highest suicide rate in Europe after Sweden; they're throwing themselves off buildings and under reindeer just to get away from the bloody place.

PALIN: (*Offended.*) There's no need be Norwegianist.

CHAPMAN: Oh, this is ridiculous. I can't stay here all day defending a film that was perfectly well intentioned.

PALIN: (*Normal voice.*) Well, there is the interval.

CHAPMAN: I'm sorry?

PALIN: There is the interval. You can put your feet up.

CHAPMAN: You're not supposed to mention that.

PALIN: Why not?

CHAPMAN: It's not the done thing.

PALIN: Says who?

CHAPMAN: It's a theatrical convention. You're not supposed to break the 4th wall and let the audience know that you know you're performing.

PALIN: What wall?

CHAPMAN: The wall over there: between us and the audience.

PALIN: I can't see a wall.

CHAPMAN: It's invisible.

PALIN: You're taking the piss. (*Scoffs.*) Wall.

CHAPMAN: I'll show you.

CHAPMAN and PALIN cross to the front of the stage; CHAPMAN mimes pressing his hands against an invisible wall.

See?

PALIN: You're just doing a very bad mime. What are you, French?

CHAPMAN: It's a wall I tell you.

PALIN: Wall my arse.

CHAPMAN: It's there.

PALIN: I'll prove it's not.

CHAPMAN: How?

PALIN: I'll run at it.

CHAPMAN: I wouldn't do that if I were you.

PALIN: Why not?

CHAPMAN: You might get hurt.

PALIN: Bollocks.

PALIN runs at the invisible wall, mimes as if he has come up against a solid object and lands flat on his back.

No, you're right, there's a wall. I'm in considerable pain. Thank God it's nearly the interval –

Lights cross fade to:

Music: dramatic Alfred Hitchcock thriller style strings plays.

A huge neon sign at the back of the stage flashes: 'INTERVAL!' in glowering red.

Lights rise on:

CHAPMAN entering as Alan Whicker and addressing the audience, carrying a microphone:

CHAPMAN: And so we say farewell to Act One of Pythonsesque: an over-reverential but well meaning excursion into the likes, the loves and the labours of the Monty Python team; a group of over-educated smart-arses who took the 1970's and the world by storm.

He exits and IDLE enters as David Frost, and addresses the audience, carrying a microphone:

IDLE: Act One was super, the audience were super, Eric Idle was super but most of all I, David Frost, was super. In Act Two they deal with the *Life of Brian* and its supposed attack on the myths and legend of Christ. Who was also super – if cruel to fish; he couldn't walk past a live fish without clubbing it to death; would bite a head off a fish for a bet at parties. Would always turn the other cheek – but not with fish.

With fish the man was an animal but I digress: now it's nearly time for the interval which will be super; you're super, life's super, the show is super but most of all I, David Frost, television colossus and media Zeus, am super. That's all from me, that's all from you, exit left David Frost, looking, feeling and acting – super.

As IDLE exits CLEESE enters as an urgently speaking Royal correspondent, carrying a microphone:

CLEESE: Good evening, I'm Stanley Kowalski, your royal correspondent. I'm reporting to you from outside Buckingham Palace where her majesty the queen waits in hushed anticipation for the interval to begin; that most un-royal of social occasions when she can nip to the bog and have a crafty fag like the rest of us mere mortals. (*Goes into a crazed rant.*) God I hate this job, royal watcher?

Who wants to watch a bunch of balding chinless wonders, living off the British taxpayer like a great festering leech, suck English society dry while there are people starving in Frinton? Burn it all down, that's what I say: all the palaces and grovelling toadies and senile, bed wetting lords and incontinent barons who make this country look like a Ruritanian feudal backwater from a fucking Tintin book. Take them all out, every one of the swine; one revolver, back of the neck, laughing and giggling; just like the Romanoff's. (*Pulls himself together.*) I do apologise. The heroin I smoked just before this broadcast is beginning to kick in, back to Gavin in the studio. (*Tiny Tim from* A Christmas Carol *voice.*) Merry Christmas M. Scrooge and God bless us each and every one.

The lights cross fade to:

PALIN sitting at a desk dressed as a newsreader; he addresses the audience:

PALIN: Thank you, Stanley, and finally before the interval, a round up of tonight's news: in a surprising development in the Spanish General Election General Francisco Franco, fascist dictator, has been re-elected to power, despite being dead since 1975. The Generalissimo was not available for comment but reports can confirm he still has the erection. In the Middle East peace broke out on the Gaza Strip today when Hamas decided to stage their own all naked version of *Fiddler on the Roof* using 1,037 veiled dancing girls and Topol's Arab brother-in-law Nigel. There were three deaths reported at the National Theatre tonight as the Rumanian dancing bear Otto, appearing in the Patrick Marber play *Dealer's Choice*, broke out of character, ignored the 4th wall and mauled members of the Arts Council sitting in the front row; for their withdrawal of funding for the Rumanian squirrel delegation's production of *Death of a Salesman*. In sport: England 0, One Legged Long John Silver's 7. So an improvement for the England football team there, under the new management of Sicilian boss-of-bosses/don-of-dons Luigi 'I not only sleep with the fishes I have sex with the fishes' Garibaldi. Finally, this just in, a huge foot has been seen in the vicinity of BBC Television Centre crushing passers-by and stamping large sections of the crowd at the Queen's Park Rangers stadium in Shepherd's Bush. Police advise anyone supporting Queen's Park Rangers to seek psychiatric help as soon as is humanly possible. But enough about my sexual foibles; that's between me, my therapist and the hooker on the Edgware Road, in the Viking helmet, who beats me to within an inch of my life using tinsel Tuesdays and sometimes Thursday. Time for the –

At this moment a huge polystyrene foot descends and crushes PALIN as he sits reading the news.

A snap blackout.

Music: a speeded up version of 'Tiptoe Through The Tulips' by Tiny Tim.

The music stops abruptly as if a needle has been snatched away from the record.

End of Act One.

Act Two

The lights dim for the start, we presume, of Act Two; the audience settle.
Suddenly IDLE enters down the theatre aisle (picked out by a spotlight),
ranting to members of the audience:

IDLE: Theatre? Don't talk to me about theatre. With
its surly ushers, fresh out of drama school, sullenly
selling you programmes because they can't get proper
jobs; programmes written by failed playwrights from
Croydon with dyslexia; in musty auditoriums filled with
over-dressed snobs sitting pompously through plays by
Alan Ayckbourn and his relentless satires on the suburban
middle classes with someone always being goosed in
the wood shed whilst the central character swigs sherry
like a deranged wino and swaps hate-filled domestic
quips with his saggy breasted, drink sozzled spouse. Or
Shakespearean plays with big jessie's mincing about
the stage, clad in tights and codpieces, pretending they
actually understand the inane dialogue, declaiming 17th
century gibberish in loud, hammy voices in front of fat
arsed Finnish female exchange students forced to attend
as its part of the school syllabus who spend the whole time
giggling, eating crisps and ogling the juvenile lead even
though he's patently been gay since the womb. Or Pinter
plays with his menacing strangers being menacing time
after time after time after bloody time, with their pregnant
pauses – pause after pause after pause after bloody pause;
and the moth-eaten rows of seating that were designed
for undernourished Victorians with very short legs; and
the theatre bars at the interval where you get a warm G
& T in a lipsticked-smudged glass for seventeen pounds
ninety-four served to you by a balding, embittered git in a
white nylon shirt still bitter he never got into acting school
in 1976 because he failed his audition by singing 'I Will
Survive' in a Brechtian manner who resents you asking for
ice even though it's a hundred and seven degrees in the

foyer; a foyer filled with blue-rinsed old ladies, resentful they've lost their sex drive, jostling you at the sweet counter, hogging the ice creams, tutting at your clothing and muttering nasty things about letting in the working classes and there ought to be a cull of the proletariat just because you have the audacity to come to the theatre wearing jeans; bemoaning *Cats* isn't on anymore and whatever happened to the new playwrights? Playwrights who write plays they wouldn't go and see in a million bloody years; and the coach parties from Wellingborough and St Albans full of brain dead, fat thighed provincials, stuffing their bloated, bovine faces with Snickers, Twix's or Diet Coke, only in town to watch shows with Abba medleys, soap stars or Joseph and his amazing Technicolor fucking dream-coat –

IDLE exits through an exit door still talking;

In the darkness the voice of CLEESE is heard, playing a BBC announcer:

CLEESE: And now on BBC 2, a change to the advertised programme on sheep herding: (*Gossipy.*) the sheep turned nasty apparently, something to do with Chernobyl, savaged the dog, killed the farmer, his wife, entire family, half the village; they had to call in the army, they were worrying tanks by the end, wholesale slaughter, blood everywhere, (*Sobs.*) I've never seen anything like it – oh, the humanity, the humanity. (*Pulls himself together.*) But now for something subtly different.

Lights cross-fade to:

CHAPMAN and PALIN at the pearly gates, dressed in white.

CHAPMAN: It's not right.

PALIN: That's life, brother.

CHAPMAN: I'm dead.

PALIN: That's death, brother.

CHAPMAN: I came here in good faith.

PALIN: No, you didn't, you came here because you were dead.

CHAPMAN: Look, isn't there anyone superior to you?

PALIN: Oh, superior, he says. Someone working class isn't good enough for you, eh?

CHAPMAN: I didn't mean that –

PALIN: I'm too blue collar, plebeian, merely a worker ant, a drone, just shit beneath your shoe, you oppressive Tory git.

CHAPMAN: Look, just get me someone in authority.

PALIN: I will. You'll see. He'll sort you out, you bloody snob.

CHAPMAN: I am not a snob.

PALIN: Lord Snooty, that's what I'm calling you from now on.

CHAPMAN: Oh, be quiet.

PALIN: Here he is: he'll soon put you in your place.

CHAPMAN: Who will?

CLEESE enters dressed as a pope.

CLEESE: You bastard.

PALIN & CHAPMAN: (*Together.*) Pope Pious XII!

Music: a burst of dramatic music.

CLEESE: You've got a nerve.

PALIN: Alright your holiness?

CLEESE: No, I'm not alright, I was snogging a stigmatic, as you do, when Saint Francis of Assisi runs in, fondling a badger, and tells me this atheistic arse-wipe is actually trying to get into heaven.

CHAPMAN: When I said I wanted someone in authority I didn't mean a dead pope.

CLEESE: Well, you're not going get a live one up here, mush.

CHAPMAN: Then you'll have to do: look, I'm fed up of this endless debate on the *Life of Brian*.

CLEESE: Of course there's an endless debate. It was a vicious satire on the holiest story of them all: the nativity and the crucifixion of our lord.

CHAPMAN: What's this, moral outrage?

CLEESE: Too bloody right it is.

CHAPMAN: Where was that in World War II when you never raised a single protest against the actions of the Italian fascists or the German Nazis?

CLEESE: Once more a virulent attack on the Catholic Church; don't you people ever get tired of Papist bashing? 'Every Sperm is Sacred', that jaunty little ditty went down like a lead bleeding balloon up here, mate.

CHAPMAN: Actually we were wildly contemptuous of the bigots in the Protestant Church too.

CLEESE: Ha-ha! So you admit the *Life of Brian* was an attack on organised religion?

CHAPMAN: Brian, Brian, Brian; that's all I've heard since I got here. How come no one ever talks about the Holy bloody Grail?

PALIN: Now he's blaspheming the Holy Grail!

CLEESE: Blasphemer!

CHAPMAN: Not the actual Holy Grail, the Monty Python film *The Holy Grail*.

CLEESE: Oh, blaspheme the sacred chalice from the last supper as well, why don't you? I don't see you pouring scorn on Islam do I? Haven't got the balls for it, have you, mush? They'd slap a fatwah on your arse faster than you could say Salman Rushdie.

CHAPMAN: *The Holy Grail* was a mockery of the Arthurian legend not religion. The woman in the lake, Camelot and all that; (*Chuckles.*) actually, there's rather an amusing anecdote about the coconuts –

CLEESE: (*Baffled.*) Coconuts, what fucking coconuts?

Lights cross fade to:

GILLIAM enters at a gallop, dressed as a Middle Ages serf, beating two coconuts shells together; he stops when he sees the audience. He speaks directly to them:

GILLIAM: You're probably wondering about the coconuts. No, me neither. After the 4th series of the show finished we decided, Eric in particular, that the shows just weren't the same without John. So we decided not to do any more television. We'd kind of exhausted the sketch format anyway. Something extraordinary had happened however. The records had become a cult success in the States leading to the shows being shown on Public Service Broadcasting. We became wildly popular Stateside almost overnight. So much so we were offered the chance to do a movie. We'd already put together a compilation of the best sketches *And Now For Something Completely Different* for the American market but sketches hadn't really worked. We needed a theme. Terry Jones and I were obsessed with the Middle Ages and all things covered in shit so the Arthurian legend seemed to be the logical choice. *The Holy Grail* was a huge hit in the States; Python mania had begun. Our lives were never the same. Why the coconuts? On our budget we couldn't afford horses. (*Mock English accent.*) Last one to the court of the limp-wristed Saxon King is a leper!

GILLIAM exits galloping and beating the coconut shells together.

Cross fade to:

CLEESE stands standing ramrod straight and awkward in a bowler hat; he addresses the audience:

CLEESE: Good evening, this is a pointless link. It is a link
without either comic purpose or theatrical point. It is
indeed a link with no artistic reason whatsoever. I'm sure
you're expecting japery, drollery, satire, sarcasm, irony,
mirth or pratfalls – any minute now. Unfortunately the
writer has scraped the bottom of the comedic barrel.
There's no jokes left at the inn. No pantomime puns.
No slapstick shtick. Nothing left alive in that town called
Chuckles. So here I stand. Without lame one-liners for
a crutch; filling a meaningless vacuum whilst the actor
playing Terry Gilliam changes into a costume to play Eric
Idle; as if any of us here tonight could tell the fucking
difference; (*Sighs.*) very well, you've forced me against my
will, to tell what working class people so laughingly call 'a
joke.' (*Clears his throat.*) How many Freudians does it take
to change a light-bulb? Two: one to change the light-bulb,
the other to hold the penis...ladder...ladder. (*Beat.*) No, I
didn't find it funny either. But one man's ceiling is another
man's floor. As one woman's bathroom is often another
woman's toilet, if that woman is vulgar and from a council
estate. And now to kill myself rather than spout any more
of this drivel.

*CLEESE attempts to hang himself using his own tie; a snap
blackout.*

In the darkness: the sound of a gunshot.

Lights cross-face to:

*IDLE playing a film reviewer of the smug, self-satisfied kind; JONES
sits opposite him playing a lecherous Italian film director.*

IDLE: Hello, and welcome to *Cinema Now*: an incredibly
pompous arts programme for incredibly pompous people.
Tonight to discuss with me the film *Monty Python & The Holy
Grail* is leading Italian director Federico Pascolini. Auteur
and director, of course, of those classics of post-war Italian
cinema: *The Many Lusts of Lucretia Borgia* and *Death Gets a
Stiffy*. Federico, was the film to your taste?

JONES: On the contrary I found it, how you say in
   English, anal.

IDLE: I'm sorry, could you define what you mean by 'anal.'

JONES: It was so repressed, so English, so lacking in passion.
   Where were the women? Where was the fornication?
   Where was the writhing, naked bodies thrashing about
   in mud? The chastity belts snapping as sex crazed monks
   debauch themselves like gluttonous satyrs on wine and
   the local courtesans with the Black Death and the heaving
   mammary glands?

IDLE: Well, not every film can be about sex, Federico –

JONES: Of course every film should be about sex, life is about
   sex; King Arthur did not ravish one woman in the whole
   of the film. Where were the shots of the boobies? It was a
   sensual age; there were filthy boobies where ever a man
   looked. Coconuts, I laugh in your English face, what are
   coconuts compared to sweating, bouncing boobies?

IDLE: Could we possibly move on from the subject of sexuality
   and discuss the comic masterstroke that was the Knights
   of Ni –

JONES: What kind of knights want shrubbery, knights want to
   fornicate, without the shrubbery; cactus maybe but never
   shrubbery. What is phallic about shrubbery? Nothing;
   I despise you, English person, and I despise you to
   your face. Without phallic symbolism a film is turd, less
   than turd.

IDLE: I really feel we should move on from the sexual debate,
   Federico. *Holy Grail* is not really a sensuous, art house
   movie. It's a comedy mocking Hollywood's version of the
   Middle Ages.

JONES: Yes, like *El Cid*.

IDLE: Quite, yes, like *El Cid*.

56

JONES: Sophia Loren was in *El Cid*. And for vast parts of the movie all you could see were her magnificent melons. The camera never left her melons; you could hardly see El Cid's head for her melons. His noggin was like a pin it was so small in comparison to her melons. This is cinema to me.

IDLE: Hang about, what about the scene in Castle Anthrax where one hundred and fifty scantily clad vestal virgins try and seduce the chaste Sir Galahad, played with frightening intensity by Michael Palin; shot in 1970's porn movie soft focus? That was phallic.

JONES: Vestal virgins? I sneer contemptuously in your face, English person. They did not show their boobs, their bazooms, their knockers, their jugs, their Bristol's, their bazookas, their Charlie's, their titties, their bazongas, their norks, their dingle-berries –

IDLE: (*Embarrassed.*) Alright, Federico, alright, let's leave *The Holy Grail*; let's review *Last Tango in Paris* shall we?

JONES: Not enough sex.

IDLE: Oh, come on, the whole movie is one long erotic encounter.

JONES: I felt Brando could have used more butter in the buttocks scene.

IDLE: You're sex obsessed.

JONES: I'm Italian: it goes with the turf.

IDLE: This is ridiculous; you can't dismiss every film because they're not overtly pornographic.

JONES: (*Coughs.*) Anal.

IDLE: I am not anal.

JONES: (*Coughs.*) Anal.

IDLE: Stop it.

JONES: (*Coughs.*) Anal.

IDLE: I'm warning you –

The lights cross fade to:

CLEESE addressing the audience, as himself:

CLEESE: In 863 A D King Malcolm the Murky, lord of the rampaging Celtic hordes, conquered the lesser known regions of Cumbria by attacking the locals with curling tongs. In 1836, at the siege of the Alamo, Davy Crockett, last of the great frontiersmen, was killed by a sexually demented raccoon who mistook his hat for its mate. Neither of the aforementioned facts are connected but it just goes to show how your mind wanders when you're bored; the idea for the *Life of Brian* came where we were promoting *Holy Grail* in Europe. Eric said the next movie should be called Jesus Christ – Lust For Glory. This made us all fall about and we dutifully went off to research Biblical history. It became pretty clear right away that a mocking of Christ was not on. How are you going to mock someone you agree with wholeheartedly? So the idea was to have the story of a guy who was around at the same time as Jesus. Who was mistaken for a miracle worker. We were taking the piss out of left wing guerilla organisations, trade unions, followers of false religious cults and zealots everywhere. We were certainly not doing Jesus down. Unfortunately EMI thought otherwise. They were with us all the way to finance the film – until they actually read the script.

Cross fade to:

PALIN plays a Lord Delfont style figure (chairman of EMI and showbiz impresario) figure who sits opposite CHAPMAN and IDLE, playing themselves.

CHAPMAN: But EMI said they wanted to finance our next movie.

PALIN: That was before we saw what you'd written.

IDLE: What's wrong with it?

PALIN: What's right with it? You've done something remarkable: you've managed to offend Christians, Jews and Muslims all at the same time.

CHAPMAN: No we haven't.

PALIN: On the contrary, you're achieved something that no one else has done in 2000 years of religious conflict: you've brought all the major religions together – they're all pissed off.

CHAPMAN: I thought you were keen to give us artistic freedom.

PALIN: Not this much artistic freedom.

CHAPMAN: There should be no limit to artistic freedom.

PALIN: There is if it costs me money.

CHAPMAN: Why won't you make money?

PALIN: Who'd come and see it? Save for deranged atheists. The general public will stay away in droves.

IDLE: You underestimate the intelligence of the public.

PALIN: I didn't get where I am today by over-estimating the intelligence of the public. Can't you just go back to being wacky about the middle ages?

CHAPMAN: We've done that, we're moving on.

PALIN: So am I. The door is the wooden bit in the wall. Go, and never darken my carpets again.

IDLE: Frankly, I'm very disappointed in EMI.

PALIN: We've just lost a fortune on the Sex Pistols. The bastards vomited and swore all over this office; whatever happened to professionalism? You'd never have Tony Bennett behave like that. He vomits and swears in the privacy of his own home.

CHAPMAN: You can't go back on your word.

PALIN: I can, I have and I will. To paraphrase the Bible: in the beginning was the word and the word was 'no'. Excuse me; I'm late for my weekly arm wrestle with Sir Lew Grade.

PALIN exits.

CHAPMAN: So what'll we do now?

IDLE: (*Michael Caine impression.*) Hang about: I've got an idea.

CHAPMAN: Eric, why are you talking like that?

IDLE: I was doing Michael Caine.

CHAPMAN: Now's not the time for pointless impressions.

IDLE: George, we can go to George.

CHAPMAN: George who?

IDLE: The George.

CHAPMAN: What, the pub?

IDLE: No, the Beatle.

A snap blackout.

Music: a folk-quartet sing 'The Leaving of Liverpool.'

The voice of JONES is heard, doing a cod travel documentary voice:

JONES: Liverpool, city of dreams, with a higher crime rate per square inch than San Quentin; what do you call a Liverpudlian's push-bike? Stolen. What do you call a Liverpudlian in a suit? A burglar on the way to his wedding; but from this most unfashionable and un-fabulous of cities came the fabulous four: The Beatles. John, Paul, George and – the passenger. Who between 1962 and 1970 came to rule the world with their mop-tops and their loveable Scouser ways; but where does a Beatle go when the dream is over? What hobbies does he take up?

In George Harrison's case it was gardening, collecting gnomes and befriending Eric Idle. It was this quasi-mystic, India obsessed, banjo-playing fanatic who became the Python's unlikely saviour.

Music: harp music plays 'All You Need Is Love'.

Lights cross fade to:

IDLE enters as George Harrison in a large, ridiculously fake beard.

The music fades.

IDLE address audience:

IDLE: Hello, I'm George Harrison. And it's really gear to be talking to you tonight. I thought it'd be grotty but it's really, really gear. What am I talking about? I've absolutely no idea. I'd just like to thank the house band for playing 'All You Need Is Love' as I came on, a song patently written by John Lennon and not me. It reminds me of when Frank Sinatra used to sing my song: 'Something'. He'd introduce it in concert with: 'and now the most beautiful love song ever written, by two young men called Mr Lennon and Mr McCartney.' Cheers Frank, Mafia twerp. When Eric came to me and told me about EMI's decision not to back the movie I told him I'd finance it instead. Why? I was a huge fan of the show and I wanted to see the movie. It was the most expensive film ticket in history. I set up Handmade films and raised two million. I was as surprised as everyone else by the fuss the film raised. Of course, I was used to bigots getting the wrong end of the stick. In '66 John told a reporter some kids thought The Beatles to be bigger than Christ. The American religious South went gaga and burnt our records. The Dave Clark Five and Freddie & the Dreamers should have had their records burnt. But that's for being crap not sacrilegious; was the *Life of Brian* offensive? I wouldn't have backed it if it were. If I didn't respect other religions who did? But I can't stop. I've got a banjo convention to attend in Blackpool. (*He exits singing.*)

'Oh, Mr Woo, what can I do, for Mr Woo's a window cleaner now.'

A blackout.

In the blackout the voice of PALIN:

PALIN: (*Australian accent.*) And now an advertisement for the Australian tourist board; (*Wistful.*) Oh, Australia: where every man is free to be prime minister…provided he's a mason…and not foreign…or throws a boomerang…or is a woman…ah, Australia…the outback…the Sydney Harbour Bridge…the lager vomit…the land where men are men, billabongs are billabongs and soap operas are moronic…

Music: a recording of 'Waltzing Matilda', which is then ripped violently from the turn-table.

Lights rise on:

CHAPMAN, CLEESE, IDLE and PALIN sit in Australian bush hats with corks hanging from them; drinking from tins of Fosters Lager. They play Australians during the following:

IDLE: Save for being Pommy bastards there's nothing wrong with the Monty Python team per say.

CLEESE: Except they dress like Sheila's.

PALIN: Right, you wouldn't get an Australian bloke dressing up as a woman just to get cheap laughs.

CHAPMAN: Perish the thought, mate. Rolf Harris wearing a third leg whilst playing his didgeridoo certainly but you'd never see Rolf dress up as a girl.

PALIN: He's too busy tying down kangaroos and doing unfeasible things to them.

CHAPMAN: But always in a most manly way. Of course all Pommies are, and this is not meant to be offensive in any way, poofs.

IDLE: Right, even the heterosexuals.

CLEESE: Poofs to a girl – and the girls.

CHAPMAN: Most of all – they never stop whinging.

PALIN: Right, you wouldn't catch an Australian whinging. Alright, we're still whining about the 1931 'Bodyline' cricket tour –

CHAPMAN: And Gallipoli –

IDLE: And when the English cheated to win the Rugby World Cup –

CLEESE: They kept kicking the ball over the post, the cheating bastards.

PALIN: But you'd never hear an Australian whine otherwise. Certainly we're over-confident –

CLEESE: Over hearty –

IDLE: Over bearing –

CHAPMAN: And over here –

PALIN: But bar that? We're perfect.

CLEESE: (*Beat.*) Yet never smug.

PALIN: You wouldn't catch an Australian being smug. Even though, as you and I know, we come from the greatest country in the world with the best weather and best bouncing rodents.

CHAPMAN: How many countries, after all, can boast an egg laying mammal?

CLEESE: Only us.

IDLE: (*Wistful.*) I had sex once with an egg laying mammal.

They all turn and stare at IDLE.

Oh, I'm sorry did I say that out loud?

CHAPMAN: Where were we?

PALIN: Talking about the Monty Python team, funny bastards.

CHAPMAN: Funny as hell.

PALIN: Even if they're not as funny bastards as funny Australian bastards.

CLEESE: I do take umbrage at their mockery and hostility towards Australian table wines however.

IDLE: You're not wrong there, mate.

CLEESE: I know I'm not wrong.

PALIN: No Australian is ever wrong.

CHAPMAN: They could be cab drivers they're never wrong so often.

IDLE: And never wrong loudly.

CLEESE: Alright, in the 1970's drinking Australian table wine was like drinking sheep dip steeped in urine. It was thought low brow and vulgar by the European bourgeoisie. But those days are long gone.

CHAPMAN: You're right there, mate.

CLEESE: Not only am I right but I'm also not wrong. Today Australian table wines are found in the homes of most complacent middle class families in suburbs of places as varied as London, Paris, Cape Town or Grimsby.

IDLE: Now brand names such as Lindeman's, Jacob's Creek, Hardy's and Rawnsley Estate are guzzled regularly by domestic binge drinkers who swill it like there's no tomorrow. The first glass is sipped but as the evening progresses and they realize their lives are an empty sham of nothingness they start swigging it by the neck and yelling at their wife and kids that they've ruined their entire life and that without them holding them back they might have succeeded in their childhood dream of becoming an international porn star in exotic Swedish skin flicks with girls called Elke sucking their great big pink –

All the others stare at IDLE. He stops embarrassed.

Oh, I'm sorry did I say that out loud?

A huge pause, then:

CLEESE: Of course, as an Australian, you're not wrong.

The others ad-lib agreement. A snap blackout.

In the darkness the voice of IDLE playing a BBC television announcer:

IDLE: And that was this week's episode of *Skippy The Bush Kangaroo*. Where Skippy unfeasibly saved a nuclear power plant from an infestation of killer bees; the producers would like to point out that only three kangaroos were killed in the making of this television programme. Oh, and a koala bear, and the ostrich that got eaten by the crew. And the duck billed platypus the producer ran over whilst pissed; and all the bees. But now it's that time of night when tedium, religious intolerance and blind bigotry combine – yes, it's the Epilogue, with the right reverend Terry Jones.

In the darkness the voice of JONES, playing a vicar:

JONES: And, yea, Jesus walked forth from Galilee and moved to Norway and became a Viking –

IDLE: What do you mean, Jesus was a Viking?

JONES: Well, he might have been.

IDLE: He was Jewish.

JONES: They had Jewish Vikings.

IDLE: When? What was the Jewish Viking motto then? They Burn, They Pillage, They Shop? You just try and squeeze bloody Vikings into everything.

JONES: No, I don't.

IDLE: Last week you said Jesus turned water into mead.

JONES: So I'm obsessed with Vikings. Is it a crime?

IDLE: It is during the epilogue. Now do a proper one.

JONES: Sorry, sorry. (*Religious tone.*) And, yea, the twelve disciples sat down to the last supper and they had chicken and a roasting pig with an apple in it's mouth and Judas started singing sea shanties in Norwegian as the others quaffed lager. 'Let's invade England' a gruff voice bellowed. 'Last one to the fjord is a sissy!' And, yea, Jesus put on his Norse helmet and picked up his axe and yelled: 'Let's slaughter some Geordies!' Hussah they belched. And yea, the Norsemen slaughtered many English, laying waste to the land, for many centuries, until Abba formed and they decided to do West End musicals instead –

The voice fades.

Lights rise on:

PALIN and CHAPMAN, dressed in white, at the pearly Gates;

PALIN: That George Harrison will be in trouble when he gets here.

CHAPMAN: What, for playing the banjo?

PALIN: No, for financing that film.

CHAPMAN: He was only trying to help.

PALIN: We had enough trouble with that John Lennon.

CHAPMAN: Why, what did he do?

PALIN: Sat in Jesus' chair.

CHAPMAN: At least he got in. This after singing 'imagine there's no heaven'. What did I do? Just play the lead in a comedy movie. Where I come from you're innocent until proven guilty.

PALIN: Hark at the barrack room lawyer.

CHAPMAN: I demand a trial.

PALIN: This isn't the Spanish Inquisition.

A huge pause; they both wait for something dramatic to happen: nothing.

Maybe not, right, well, you'd better have a trial then.

A snap blackout.

Music: court-room drama music plays.

In the darkness the voice of IDLE is heard, doing a rapid American accent:

IDLE: Yes, the court-room, where men go to be judged and shysters go to hide; inspiring movies as sweaty as: *Twelve Angry Men, To Kill a Mocking Bird* and *Judgment at Nuremburg.* Where sweaty men in sweaty white suits get incredibly pompous and/or sweaty whilst judging others less sweaty than themselves; who can forget the 'Monkey Trial' with Clarence Darrow, as played by Spencer Tracy, nobly defending the right of monkeys to teach Darwin whilst defecating on schoolroom floors? Who can forget Raymond Burr as Perry Mason? Despite the fact most of us have? We take you to that British institution – the Old Bailey. Where justice is doled out like hot sperm at an orgy. (*Beat.*) My God, I feel horny…

Lights rise on:

A courtroom scene; CHAPMAN in the dock, PALIN a clerk of the court, CLEESE the prosecution lawyer, IDLE the high court judge.

CLEESE: Your honour I realise you're a high court judge and I wouldn't want to waste your time – you being senile, incompetent and a mason – but I must insist on pressing for the death penalty for this vile, vile, guilty bastard.

CHAPMAN: I'm already dead.

IDLE: Silence in court.

PALIN: Silence in court.

IDLE: Clerk of the court?

PALIN: Yes m'lud?

IDLE: Swear in the accused.

PALIN: Yes m'lud.

> *PALIN produces a large, black book.*

Place your hand on this Bible. Do you promise to tell the truth, the whole truth and nothing but the truth so help you God?

CHAPMAN: I do. (*Beat.*) Wait a minute, that's not a Bible; it's *Black Beauty* by Anna Sewell.

PALIN: No it's not.

CHAPMAN: Yes it is. I can see a picture of the horse on the cover.

PALIN: Not my fault. We've had a lot of Liverpudlians in the dock recently. They keep stealing the Bibles.

CHAPMAN: Will you people stop being so offensive to Liverpudlians? It's regionalist. And your treatment of Canadians is downright racist.

CLEESE: Yes, but comedy needs a victim. (*Northern accent.*) I'm not saying my mother-in-law's ugly but when she goes swimming in Lock Ness the monster gets out and pickets the lake.

CHAPMAN: You'll be doing misogynist jokes from the 1970's next.

CLEESE: (*Northern accent.*) Did you hear about the lesbian who put her finger in the dyke and saved Holland?

CHAPMAN: Objection: that was sexism and homophobia of the highest order.

IDLE: Sustained.

CLEESE: I'm sorry, my lord, I had a flashback to Batley Variety Club in 1973.

> (*Northern accent.*) When chicken in the basket were king. (*Normal voice.*) May I press on?

IDLE: Feel free to press on.

PALIN: Can I press on?

IDLE: Silence in court; open your case for the prosecution, Mr Kipling.

CLEESE: Thank you, m'lud. Graham Ethel Merman Chapman –

CHAPMAN: My middle names are not Ethel and Merman.

CLEESE: Graham Tarka the Otter Chapman –

CHAPMAN: I'm not called that either. This is outrageous.

CLEESE: Graham Albert Tatlock Ena Sharples Jacques Brel Chapman –

CHAPMAN: Will you stop calling me these silly names?

CLEESE: Answer the question: yes or no.

CHAPMAN: You haven't asked me a question.

CLEESE: (*With rising aggression.*) Were you or were you not on that grassy knoll on November 22nd 1963? Did you or did you not deliberately place an iceberg in the way of The Titanic on December 12th 1912? When they were changing the guard at Buckingham Palace did you, with extreme and deliberate malice, go down to the palace with Alice?

> Did you go out of your way to win the 1977 Grand National dressed as the rear end of a panto pit pony whilst claiming, quite illegally, to be the racehorse Shergar? Are you not, in fact, as is clear to everyone in this court-room, actually the 1950's smarmy vaudeville entertainer Frankie 'Give Me The Moonlight' Vaughan?

CHAPMAN: These questions have nothing to do with the *Life of Brian*.

CLEESE: I'll be the judge of that.

IDLE: No, I'll be the judge of that.

PALIN: Can I be the judge of that?

IDLE: Silence in court; continue please, Mr Kipling.

CLEESE: I put it to you, Mr Chapman, that in forty-five television episodes, four films and eleven albums – including compilations and all available for sale in the foyer of this very theatre – you set out with your sneering, over-educated colleagues to mercilessly ridicule, mock and undermine the very British society that spawned you?

CHAPMAN: Of course we did; we were comic writers and performers. To paraphrase Michael Palin's favourite quote: 'the world is a looking glass and gives back to every man the reflection of his own face. Frown at it, and it will in turn look sourly upon you; laugh at it, and it is a jolly, kind companion.'

CLEESE: What kind of bollocks is that?

CHAPMAN: Palin believes it and he's the nicest man alive, after Nelson Mandela.

CLEESE: Yes, but Mandela could take Palin in a scrap.

CHAPMAN: No, he couldn't.

CLEESE: Yes, he could. Mandela used to break rocks. He was in prison for twenty-seven years. He could kick Palin's skinny white arse, big time.

CHAPMAN: Palin's from Sheffield; they're men of steel. After all, as a child, he wrestled the school bear.

CLEESE: No, he didn't. Mandela could bite his goolies off.

IDLE: Silence in court; I declare this trial invalid.

CLEESE: Why? I was this far away from convicting the bastard.

IDLE: Yes, but its time for the cheese shop parody.

CLEESE: Must we, m'lud? Must we cover every cliché?

IDLE: A homage is not a cliché.

PALIN: Isn't homage a type of cheese?

CHAPMAN: How many references to the next sketch do you need?

IDLE: Silence in court. (*Camp voice.*) Ooo, and if I say that again I'll scream.

PALIN: Cab for fake cheese sketch! Cab for fake cheese sketch!

FX: The sound of a speeding cab pulling up.

A snap blackout.

The voice of IDLE is heard, doing an exaggerated French accent:

IDLE: Ah, cheese. It was invented by a Frenchman, you know. What he was doing with that cow's udder is anybody's business but he was French all the same; the English with their cheeses, I spit. Who names a cheese after a gorge? What the hell is a gorge now you come to mention it, a form of lizard? I think I might have wrestled one of those once; but only for sexual purposes and I did leave some money on the dresser. Oh, yes, the English sneer because the French eat horse and frogs legs. But what do they eat? Fish, chips and mushy peas; no wonder they are flatulent, obese and homosexual generally. The Beatles? Ha, the French have much better rock and roll bands.

There's…eh…and….eh….okay, we're not great at rock and roll. But we have Jacques Brel…alright, he's Belgian. Edith Piaf – the bandy legged singing prostitute – we have her. Vera Lynn? Petula Clark? I spit. Well, not literally. That would be disgusting; like being German. But now for the Cheese Shop Parody; (*Mutters.*) merde, it was funnier in the original French.

Lights rise on:

PALIN as a shifty, working class shop-keeper again; CLEESE enters.

CLEESE: Excuse me is this the shop where one might purchase CD's of a comedic bent?

PALIN: Sometimes.

CLEESE: What is it other times?

PALIN: A front for a brothel; you're not a copper's nark, are you?

CLEESE: Not in the least.

PALIN: I was gored by a nark once; those antlers are vicious.

CLEESE: That's of no consequence now. I've been imprisoned in a Vietnamese prisoner of war camp since 1975 and being recently released, the bamboo pole still firmly inserted up my anus, thought I might revisit the Monty Python albums I used to find so very, very amusing in my youth. Do you happen to stock the Monty Python cannon?

PALIN: Absolutely, there's a huge call for them. They never go out of fashion do they, they're so very, very witty. Yes, surrealism never dates.

CLEESE: Goodo. Do you happen then to possess a copy of their self-titled debut?

PALIN: Not at the moment, sir.

CLEESE: Ah, well, would you have the classic 'Another Monty Python Record'?

PALIN: Very funny that one, laugh a minute, sobbed with laughter listening to that one I did.

CLEESE: Yes, but do you have it?

PALIN: Not in stock at present, sir.

CLEESE: Very well, how about 'Matching Tie and Handkerchief'?

PALIN: Ah, lovely album; got the cheese shop sketch on it, and Oscar Wilde. 'One of Shaw's, sir.' A classic of its kind.

CLEESE: I'd rather hear it myself than listen to you paraphrase it thank you.

PALIN: Sold the last one this morning, sorry sir.

CLEESE: Monty Python's Previous Record?

PALIN: Had one.

CLEESE: But?

PALIN: It got stolen, by a Liverpudlian.

CLEESE: Live at Drury Lane?

PALIN: Oh yes, got that one, absolutely.

CLEESE: Let's have it then.

PALIN: (*Ducks under counter then returns.*) Sorry, sir, the mice ate it.

CLEESE: How could mice eat a CD?

PALIN: They're very big mice, sir; actually they're iguana.

CLEESE: The Album of the Soundtrack of the Trailer of the film of *Monty Python and the Holy Grail*?

PALIN: Not much call for that one, sir.

CLEESE: Not much call? It's one of the great comedy albums of our times.

PALIN: Not in these parts, sir.

CLEESE: Monty Python Live at City Center?

PALIN: The one where they sing 'Sit On My Face and Tell Me That You Love Me'?

CLEESE: That's the one.

PALIN: Sold the last copy to the leader of the Conservative Party; this very morn.

CLEESE: You're sure you actually stock Monty Python CD's?

PALIN: Absolutely.

CLEESE: Monty Python's Contractual Obligation Album?

PALIN: No.

CLEESE: The Monty Python Instant Record Collection?

PALIN: Yes or, then again, no.

CLEESE: Monty Python Sings?

PALIN: Not anymore they don't.

CLEESE: You don't have any CD's of Monty Python at all do you?

PALIN: You haven't asked about the soundtrack to the *Meaning of Life* yet.

CLEESE: Is there any point?

PALIN: Who dares wins, sir.

CLEESE: Do you have it?

PALIN: Not in the least.

CLEESE: You've wasted my time entirely.

PALIN: That'd be the point, sir.

CLEESE: I see.

PALIN: How about a bunk up with a Chinese bint for only thirty-seven guineas instead?

CLEESE: Oh, alright then.

A snap blackout.

Music: A burst of Spaghetti Western music, which fades.

In the darkness the voice of GILLIAM:

GILLIAM: Are you sitting comfortably? Because it's time for
the story of the three bears, told in the style of a Spaghetti
Western: once upon a time, north of the Rio Grande,
a young virgin in pigtails called Amy, played by Clint
Eastwood, returned home from a bloodbath at a wedding
– skipping merrily – to find three bears sleeping in her
family's beds: Papa Bear, Mama Bear and Baby Bear,
otherwise known as Miguel; taking out the Gatling Gun
she'd borrowed from the defrocked priest next door in
return for sexual favours she let loose a tirade of bullets.
The bullets spewed forth into Papa Bear's unshaven body
in slow-mo. 'No, no, no!' he screamed. Mama Bear was
next. (*Mexican voice.*) 'You Gringo bitch, we were only
fucking hibernating,' were her last words. Finally Amy
confronted Baby Bear. 'I'm only two,' wailed the poor little
bear. (*Clint Eastwood voice.*) 'You'll never see three mother
– (*Bleep.*)' said Amy, shooting again and again, giggling
like a banshee. It took the baby bear three hours to die as
blood seeped through its tiny paws. 'Why?' whispered the
little bear. 'Why?' Amy shrugged. (*Clint Eastwood voice.*)
'Never did like fucking bears.'

*Another burst of Spaghetti Western music; the record of which is
ripped merrily from the turn-table.*

Lights rise on:

*JONES sits dressed as woman. He addresses the audience in his high
pitches voice:*

JONES: Yes, it's me again. I'm like a Greek Chorus; except I'm
not Greek, or a chorus. After Brian we decided to go back
to sketches, for the film the *Meaning of Life*. I thought it was
the best thing we did. John thought it was the worst. But we
always were chalk and cheese. I was chalk, he was cheese,
'cause his Dad was called Cheese.

Changed his name in World War One as he thought the other soldiers might take the Mickey out of him. No shit Sherlock. Of course, I know all about having a strange name. You can go the length and breadth of Wales and never meet a Jones. But I digress. After the *Meaning of Life* kicked up a stink, mainly down to my exploding fat bastard, we never worked together again. Though we talked about it enough times; after Graham kicked the bucket it didn't seem right somehow. Monty Python, after all, is a six-headed beast. Anyway, Palin was always off up a mountain with a llama. Says he was making a travel documentary with it but his wife got very suspicious. I mean, who takes a llama to the South Pole, then Poland? Always flying it first class, letting it spit all over the VIP lounge at Heathrow, taking it to Vegas, sharing the honeymoon suite. Something funny is going on, that's all I'm saying. Will the Pythons ever work together again? Well 'never say never' that's what my old Gran used to say. Mind you, she was mad. Mad as a fish, as a kipper anyway. But I digress. Yes, it's just not the same without old Graham. Only forty-eight when he shuffled off; still, there'll be laughing in heaven tonight. If he gets his tadger out and dunks it in someone's Gin & Tonic anyway. Always made me laugh; mind you, I didn't drink Gin & Tonic. Who would? Graham Chapman? I've said it before and I'll say it again: he was a very naughty boy.

The lights cross fade to:

CLEESE sitting at a desk, playing a BBC television announcer, speaking directly to the audience in an urgent voice:

CLEESE: Well, ladies and gentlemen, it's page sixty of this theatrical entertainment and still no sign of a moral. Our experts in the studio were expecting the moral at least by page forty-nine but there predictions have turned out to be wildly inaccurate; over to you, Colin.

IDLE enters carrying a microphone, and speaks directly to the audience, in a political commentator's voice:

IDLE: Thank you Jonathan yes here I am outside of the Houses of Parliament. Questions have been asked during Prime Minister's Question Time as to when the moral in Pythonesque will actually appear; should there be a moral and what form will it take; high minded platitudes about Chapman's service to all mankind or accusatory and pious accusations of a life wasted. We're hoping for some tears of a clown metaphors naturally, we're hoping for he-left-'em-laughing and died with his clown boots on clichés. But who can say, Jonathan? In this show it could go either way; back to you, naked from the waist down, in the television studio.

The lights cross fade to:

CLEESE sitting at his desk as the television presenter, addressing the audience:

CLEESE: All sides have agreed it's been a very long night. We've had laughs, we've had chuckles, on one occasion we believe a guffaw but still no tears. Still no gut wrenching and moving scenes between Chapman and a dying puppy for example; still no funeral scenes, still no weeping and gnashing of teeth. We were hoping at least for some pathos or, at least some bathos, if only we knew what 'bathos' meant; a quick word from the man in the street:

Cross fade to JONES, playing a dim witted man in the street.

JONES: How come they ain't done the Parrot Sketch proper?

Cross fade to CLEESE, playing the newsreader at his desk.

CLEESE: That was a man in the street. A moron certainly, possibly a cretin, but that's what democracy is all about: allowing the remedial to have an opinion even though that opinion is – wrong. (*Puts finger to his ear.*) News just coming in, they're ready for the moral; it's on its way. Page sixty-one and we finally have the moment when the over-emphasised point is hammered home. It's been a remarkable journey and I've glad I've shared it with you, despite being naked from the waist down, my mother thanks you, my father thanks you, my sister thanks you but most of all I thank you. Over to Graham Chapman, still remarkably, after eighty minutes of tedium, stuck in the doorway to heaven.

The lights cross fade to:

CHAPMAN waiting at the pearly gates, PALIN enters, playing the Angel Herbert.

PALIN: Well, there's good news and there's bad news.

CHAPMAN: Give me the bad news first.

PALIN: You're still dead.

CHAPMAN: And the good news?

PALIN: The management in conjuncture with the sub-committee have met and, all things considered, decided to let bygones be bygones and let you in as a fully paid up member of the angelic hordes.

CHAPMAN: That's mighty big of them.

PALIN: There is one condition. You're not to reveal yourself willy-nilly and more willy than nilly like you did in Brian.

CHAPMAN: That's it then?

PALIN: That's almost it.

CHAPMAN: Aren't I done and dusted?

PALIN: Dust anyway. But it's time to explain the significance of the pipe.

CHAPMAN: Must I?

PALIN: Clause 9, brother, there must always be a sanctimonious message in any theatrical experience.

CHAPMAN: Oh, very well –

Lights cross fade to:

CHAPMAN stands and addresses the audience:

CHAPMAN: 'Pythonesque' is an adjective pertaining to or characteristic of *Monty Python's Flying Circus*, a popular British television comedy series of the 1970's, noted especially for its absurdist or surrealist humour. As defined by the Shorter Oxford Dictionary, page 2,421. Just thought I'd better clear that up, in case there's any critics and/or Python bores watching. Now to the deep significance of the pipe: it was my crutch you see, for my shyness. I smoked it from my teenage years on. It also became, I expect, my bane. I got throat cancer, you see. It then spread to my spine and Goodnight Vienna. Of course, as I was gay, they said it was Aids. Homophobia doesn't go away. It just lurks under the surface of society, waiting to pounce, like a very cruel bear. I was proud to be gay. I was proud to conquer my alcoholism. I was proud to be a Python. I was proud to write with John. I was proud to play the lead in two of the funniest movies of all time. Regrets? Of course, we all have many. Save for Sinatra. But he's a stupid bastard. I enjoyed a full life and was loved by many. What more can a man ask, save for copious amounts of cocaine and possibly several small but willing natives from Timbuktu, catering to my every sexual whim; but enough of the moral, this isn't the epilogue. Time to end on a song. Hit me with a show tune, sweetie.

Lights cross fade to:

IDLE in a woman's wig, PALIN enters in a lumberjack shirt. Both speak in Canadian accents:

IDLE: Where have you been, Jack? You've been gone so long.

PALIN: My name's Jake, Mary.

IDLE: You see, you've been gone so long I've forgotten your name, Jock.

PALIN: I've been out in the wilderness, Mary, amongst the redwoods and beech of Canada's finest forests. Oh Canada, Canada, your natural beauty overwhelms me.

That's why I have to cut down as many of your trees as possible for profit. Of course, I never wanted to be a lumberjack –

IDLE: No John?

PALIN: No, Mary, I wanted to be a Mountie, in the Canadian Mounted Police, running down fugitives and protecting the border from Americans trying to escape from their own president. Picture it, Mary, me in a butch hat and red, manly uniform; with a shiny leather holster and underneath my baggy trousers women's underwear. The finest Toronto can provide, with a snappy lace garter and a fully upholstered bra.

IDLE: Oh, Jake, Jock, Jack, John, stay in the closet, repress your natural urges and don't leave me.

PALIN: I must leave you, Mary. I must apply for the Royal Canadian Mounted Police and take to the faraway hills and mountain ranges; arresting beaver for speeding and elk for wearing antlers in a built-up area. Yes, when you're a Mountie, nothing can keep you down.

IDLE: Please don't burst into a show tune, Jacques. You know I hate it when you do that.

PALIN: Too late, Mary, the camp show pony within me is bursting to get out.

PALIN sings: 'A Mountie Must Always Get His Man.'

PALIN: So farewell to the ladies
        Sex and making babies
        Like a beaver who must make his dam
        It's farewell to the wifey
        I'm starting a new lifey
        'Cause a Mountie must always get his man.

CLEESE and CHAPMAN enter as Mounties. They join the song.

ALL: Yes, there's no use denying

The lingerie I'm buying
Mary, one day you'll understand
And I'll soon be confessin'
To all of my cross-dressin'
'Cause a Mountie must always get his man.

ALL: Canada's my country
And Canada I love thee
But I got to wear a dress like my old Gran
Just as maple is a syrup
I'm fake-butch in a stirrup
'Cause a Mountie must always get his man.
So farewell to my Mary
I'm off to be quite fairy
Pass me a parasol and fan
For underneath this clothin'
A transvestite is a'rovin'
'Cause a Mountie must always get his man
Yes, a Mountie must always get his man.

A snap blackout;

In the darkness the voice of a suave announcer is heard, played by
IDLE:

IDLE: Well, I hope you enjoyed the show. I know I did,
very amusing. We had many celebrities in tonight who
seemed to have a marvelous time. Oh, there's Christopher
Plummer, Captain Von Trapp from *The Sound Of Music*.
Hope you didn't take the jokes against Canadian Mounties
and moose wrestling too seriously, Chris. (*Worried.*) Wait
a minute, there's Neil Young too, and Joni Mitchell. What
are you doing with those truncheons? No, please, the
writer made me say those things. He had a Canadian
girlfriend who dumped him for a singing lesbian. No,
please, no. Aaaaaaaaaaaaahh!!! (*Panic and pain.*) The pain,
please there's blood. No more. What are you doing with
my trousers? Don't de-bag me please. Give me back my

underpants. They were a gift from Stephen Sondheim. Not the scissors, Joni. They're the only genitals I've got. Please! Nooooooo!

The lights rise. Enter PALIN entering dressed as a member of the Spanish Inquisition.

He addresses the audience:

PALIN: Yes, it is I, Michael Palin stroke Terry Jones, dressed again as a member of the Spanish inquisition for no apparent reason. We, Oxford graduates alongside our fiendish American ally Terry Gilliam, have counted our lines and we have more than the Cambridge opposition of Cleese, Chapman and Idle. Victory! Victory is ours. Using the twin weapons of guile, stealth and perseverance – using the three, three weapons of guile, stealth, perseverance and cunning – using the four, four weapons of guile, stealth, perseverance, cunning and charm – using the five, five – I'll come in again.

PALIN exits. A snap blackout.

Music: 'The Liberty Bell' theme plays.

The lights rise, the CAST enter, bow and exit. The lights dim once more.

The music fades.

In the darkness the voice of an announcer is heard, played by IDLE:

IDLE: Could a Mr Brian Gumby, a Mr Brian Gumby, owner of the Mini Cooper registration X73 4JF please return the gherkin to the Soviet Union as soon as possible please; it's not a gherkin, it's a nuclear device. (*Long beat.*) Could a Mr Bond, a Mr James Bond, stop knobbing the girl doing the coats, fly to Estonia and save the world as soon as he does up his flies? Thank you.

Music: Nancy Sinatra sings 'You Only Live Twice.' The record is ripped off the turntable; then the voice of a second announcer played by CLEESE:

CLEESE: Could a Mr. Nancy Sinatra, a Mr. Nancy Sinatra, please stop singing please? People have homes to go to. And their baby-sitter is late for her glue-sniffing session. This is absolutely the end of the show.

(*Dramatic voice.*) Or is it? (*Beat.*) Yes, yes it is. (*Beat.*) I've got to get back to Cambridge for a Footlights re-union. And the gondolas; gondolas as far as the eye can see…I hate those fucking gondolas –

Music: a cheesy organ plays. The music fades. Then silence.

The End